ADVANCE PRAISE

Becoming Unstoppable is an absolutely incredible compilation that will ignite your spirit and fuel your ambitions! Each author's submission is a powerhouse of motivation, pushing you to conquer challenges and reach new heights! Get ready to feel truly unstoppable!

— DR. ROZ, FOUNDER, LOVE REVOLUTION, AND AUTHOR OF *DEBTFREEDEGREE: HOW TO GRADUATE WITHOUT STUDENT LOANS WHILE GETTING GOOD GRADES, HAVING TONS OF FUN, AND LANDING YOUR DREAM JOB!*

Becoming Unstoppable hits right at the heart. You know those moments you quietly hope you'll never have to face? These women faced them and met them with grit and grace. Their stories aren't just powerful; they're deeply human, reminding us that some endings are simply a different kind of beginning. This book will move you, shift your thinking, and, most importantly, remind you of what's possible when you take the next brave step. Get the book. Settle in. And remember what you're capable of.

— REGINA GARAY, FOUNDER, RIGHT BRAIN LOVES LEFT

Reading Anna Garrison's story, I felt her true sense of rawness, vulnerability, and honesty. The subject is heartbreaking, but I want to read more of her words as she spoke truths that resonate with so many.

— CRICKETT DOLLMAN, AVID READER, MOON LOVER

These stories highlight how strength often shows up in quiet, unexpected ways. It's the kind of book that reminds you you're not alone in the messy middle of figuring things out. I found myself nodding often, seeing myself mirrored in many of these women's experiences! It's a powerful companion for anyone navigating change, reminding you that resilience can take many different forms.

— JENNIFER CORBEAU, FOUNDER,
SPIRAL PATH JOURNEYS

At sixty, my experiences over the past six decades resonate with each chapter of the book. *Becoming Unstoppable* powerfully illustrates how we are all a work in progress—that embracing every part of the journey is what builds our character. The words within serve as a vital harbinger of the human need for interdependence—we should be helping one another succeed. It champions courage over comfort, reminds us there is always something to learn, and encourages us to dwell in possibility.

— DEBBA WHITE, DIRECTOR OF CONTENT
ENGINEERING, THE WEATHER CHANNEL, USA

Becoming Unstoppable is a book written by a group of incredibly brave women that will tap into the hearts, minds, and souls of women everywhere. It is honest, heartfelt, and quite often, unflinchingly raw and vulnerable in its storytelling. Women everywhere will be able to see themselves in the courage, tenderness, and tenacity that these brave authors have shared. This book is a must-read for you and the women you care about.

— KRISTY L. CRIPPEN, FOUNDER AND THOUGHT
PARTNER, COLLABORATIVE PARTNERS
ADMINISTRATIVE SERVICES, LLC

I wish this book would land in the hands of every woman going through a life transition. If you've ever experienced a significant challenge (and who hasn't?), the stories of women facing divorce, unexpected job loss, and other turning points will inspire you never to give up hope. The writing prompts at the end of each chapter provide a doorway into your deepest fears, secret dreams, and desires, and provide a roadmap to discovering your next chapter.

— LAURIE MORIN, AUTHOR AND BOOK DOULA

Becoming Unstoppable is a masterclass in courageous self-leadership. With unflinching honesty, it challenges us to break free from the limits of expectation and step boldly into our own power. This book isn't just a roadmap for entrepreneurs or women—it's a rallying cry for anyone standing at a crossroads, daring them to choose authenticity over approval and growth over comfort. Every page is a reminder: The journey to becoming your true self is not only possible, but also necessary. Let this book be your spark to rise, evolve, and lead your next chapter with conviction.

— LAQUINCIA NICHOLS, SPEAKER, COACH, AND
FOUNDER, EXPERIENCE-COACHING.COM

Becoming Unstoppable is full of real-life stories and how its authors overcame challenges to build the future they meant for themselves. Striking honesty, followed by prompts for reader reflection, makes the book inspirational and practical for those ready to rise.

— PAT MILLER, FOUNDER, SMALL BUSINESS
OWNERS COMMUNITY

BECOMING UNSTOPPABLE

BECOMING UNSTOPPABLE

HOW ORDINARY WOMEN
ACHIEVE EXTRAORDINARY SUCCESS

Edited by
DEBORAH KEVIN

HIGHLANDER
PRESS

*For every woman who has ever doubted her voice, dimmed her light, or stood at
the edge of her own power—
This is for you.
May you rise.
May you remember who you are.
And may you become unstoppable—not because life got easier,
but because you chose to become stronger, wiser, and more wildly,
unapologetically you.*

I am no longer accepting the things I cannot change. I am changing the things I cannot accept.

— ANGELA DAVIS

CONTENTS

ISBN: 978-1-956442-60-1
Ebook ISBN: 978-1-956442-61-8
Library of Congress: Applied For.

Published by Highlander Press
501 W. University Pkwy, Ste. B2
Baltimore, MD 21210

Cover design: Patricia Creedon
Editor: Deborah Kevin

INTRODUCTION

Ask a woman you admire to write about what makes her "unstoppable," and you'll likely be met with a look that says, *"Are you serious? Me?"* I know this because I asked many women—and that was the exact response I received from most of them.

When women look in the mirror, "unstoppable" is often the *last* word that comes to mind. As they juggle families, businesses, and the endless demands of daily life, they're usually just focused on getting through the day. Rarely do they pause to think, *"Wow, I'm amazing—I'm unstoppable!"* It's hard to feel powerful when you're running on fumes and still trying to hold it all together.

This book is a collaboration with the She Boss Café, a vibrant community of women entrepreneurs dedicated to supporting and uplifting one another. Each contributor bravely shares her journey— many of which include identity crises, unexpected setbacks, and moments of deep doubt. And yet, they persisted. Step by step, they navigated the hard stuff and emerged as the powerful women you'll meet in these pages.

Women are often the glue that holds everything and everyone together, yet we rarely give ourselves credit for all we manage to do. These stories are a testament to the strength, resilience, and unstoppable spirit that lives in every one of us. What makes these women unstoppable isn't a perfect life or a lack of struggle—it's the courage to keep going, especially when things get tough.

One of the most powerful things about sharing our stories is that, in doing so, we connect with our own strengths. Each woman in this book rediscovered her power in the process of telling her truth. She realized just how far she's come—and began to own a new identity shaped not in spite of adversity but because of it.

Our hope is that as you read these stories, you'll begin to see the unstoppable woman in yourself. You'll recognize all that you've been through and all that you've overcome. And most of all, you'll know that the very fact you're here—reading these words—means your own unstoppable journey is already underway.

So take it in. Celebrate your strength. And go forth—because you, too, are *unstoppable*.

Susan Trumpler
founder, Unstoppable Women in Business
and She Boss Café

RECLAIMING LIFE
THROUGH THE LENS

ANNA GARRISON

> *The camera is an instrument that teaches people how to see without a camera.*

— DOROTHEA LANGE

The room felt eerily quiet as I closed my laptop, the click of its lid reverberating through the stillness like a gavel striking down judgment. The faint hum of the machine faded abruptly, leaving only the sound of my uneven breaths—shallow, rapid, desperate to stabilize the chaos in my chest. Moments earlier, my husband's voice had come through the screen, cool and detached, delivering words that shattered the foundation of my life: *"You're being served with divorce papers."*

My hands trembled uncontrollably as if my body instinctively rejected the reality those words carried. My chest felt like a vice had clamped around it, the pressure unbearable and unrelenting. The air, which moments ago was neutral and ordinary, now seemed suffocatingly thick, as though I had been plunged underwater. A cascade of questions came fast and sharp, each one hitting with the precision of a dagger aimed at my most vulnerable places: *What now? How will I survive? Who am I without this life?*

My eyes roamed the room in a futile search for something—anything—that could anchor me in that moment. The pale sunlight streaming weakly through the blinds felt almost mocking in its warmth, a stark contrast to the cold despair seeping into my bones. Dust particles floated lazily in the slanted rays, their aimless drift a cruel reminder of how static my world had suddenly become. My throat was parched, constricted by emotions too raw to express. My body, weighed down by the gravity of every regret and every choice that had led to this moment, felt impossibly heavy.

And then, something broke.

It wasn't me—it was the fear. It cracked, and for the first time in what felt like an eternity, I could breathe. The panic ebbed, leaving me shaken but strangely steady. In its place came something I hadn't expected: clarity. It wasn't a comforting clarity, nor was it gentle. It felt sharp, raw, and almost violent. But it was unmistakable and undeniable.

I took a deep, shaky breath, feeling the cool air rush into my lungs. My hands, still trembling, moved to wipe away the tears that had fallen freely. My skin was damp, my chest still tight, but my mind had begun to steady. I gripped the edges of the desk, my fingers curling into the wood, grounding myself in the present moment.

I didn't have all the answers. I didn't even have a plan. But in that instant, I realized I didn't need them—not yet. What I needed, more than anything, was to take a single step forward, and then another, and then another.

I felt my body respond before my mind had fully caught up. My legs straightened as I stood, the act of rising feeling monumental, almost defiant. The sunlight hit my face as I stepped closer to the window, its warmth no longer mocking but instead a quiet reminder that the world hadn't ended, even if mine felt like it had.

When I was ready, I wrote my next chapter.

After twenty-three years of marriage, I thought I knew what my future held. My identity centered on stability and family, and I thought

I had a clear vision of how my life would unfold. But suddenly, everything I had built, everything I had planned, was no longer mine. My carefully constructed life unraveled in an instant, leaving me standing at a crossroads. The path ahead was foreign and unrecognizable.

The weight of that reality pressed down on me, but I wasn't facing it alone. As a newly single mother, I had two daughters who needed me more than ever. We had just returned to the US after five years abroad, and they were both navigating significant transitions. My youngest had just started high school, filled with nerves and anticipation, while my oldest was stepping into adulthood, beginning her college journey, and adjusting to a new chapter.

Both were at pivotal moments, looking to me for guidance and strength. Though I felt as if I were falling apart inside, I knew I couldn't let them see that. I had to show them that even when life shatters, it's possible to pick up the pieces and rebuild. I had to prove to them—and to myself—that rising again was possible.

My youngest daughter, fiercely dedicated to her soccer career, became an unexpected source of inspiration. She faced every challenge with unwavering determination, pouring herself into practices and games with an intensity that mirrored the resilience I needed to find within myself. I made it my mission to support her, cheering at games in all weather, driving to early practices and tournaments, and offering comfort after tough losses. What she didn't realize was that her dedication was teaching me as much as I was guiding her.

Meanwhile, my oldest daughter navigated the excitement and challenges of college. This new chapter was filled with self-discovery and milestones, and she often called to share her triumphs and frustrations. Each late-night conversation reminded me of the strength and resilience I wanted her to see in me—proof that no matter how uncertain life might feel, we all have the power to carve our own path.

Together, my daughters became my greatest motivators. They grounded me in the present and gave me a reason to keep moving forward, even when it felt impossible. Through their eyes, I began to see my own strength. They didn't need a mother who had all the answers; they needed a mother who was willing to try, to show up, and to keep going.

I pieced together my new life and realized that the crossroads I had feared so deeply wasn't just a place of loss—it was a place of opportunity. It was an open door to a future I hadn't planned but was now free to create. And while I was still grappling with fear and uncertainty, I knew that standing still wasn't an option.

That chapter of my life wasn't just about surviving—it was about thriving. It was about becoming the kind of woman I wanted my daughters to look up to. It was about showing them that even in the face of unimaginable change, we are capable of transformation. And in doing so, I began to find the strength to believe in my own.

In that moment of deep uncertainty, I could have so easily succumbed to fear and regret. It would have been simpler to let the pain of what I had lost pull me under like a relentless tide, dragging me into a sea of despair. But something stirred within me—a spark I didn't even know I possessed. It wasn't loud or bold; it was faint, a whisper amid the deafening noise of self-doubt and fear. But it was there. That spark whispered a message that would become the foundation of my transformation: *This isn't the end; it's the beginning.*

I sat alone in the quiet of my home, surrounded by the echoes of a life that no longer existed. My eyes landed on my camera, perched on a shelf and untouched for months. That camera had been with me through so much—family milestones, chaotic military moves, and fleeting moments of beauty amid uncertainty. It had been more than a hobby; it was a lifeline, helping me capture hope and meaning when words failed.

As I stared at the camera, I realized it could be more than a tool for preserving the past—it could be the key to my future. Photography had grounded me during life's transitions, and it could do so again. But this time, it wasn't about capturing moments of joy; it was about creating something new.

That day, I made a life-changing decision: I would turn my passion for photography into a career, a purpose, and a way to rebuild my identity. It was a leap of faith with no guarantees, but it was one I was ready to take. My camera became more than a piece of equipment; it became a symbol of hope, resilience, and the power to create something beautiful from the ashes of a broken life.

Starting a business wasn't a decision I made lightly. It was driven by necessity as much as passion. I needed to create a stable foundation for my daughters and me while showing them what perseverance looked like. With no roadmap or guidebook to follow, I stepped into uncharted territory, armed only with my camera and an unrelenting determination to succeed.

The early days were filled with long nights and relentless self-doubt. I spent countless hours on my sofa, grappling with how to market myself, find clients, and turn this dream into reality. Questions haunted me: Was I on the right path? Was this venture worth pursuing, or was I setting myself up for failure? Would anyone notice my work, let alone pay for it?

Financially, it was a constant struggle. I scraped together enough for basic equipment and a simple website, but every dollar I earned went back into the business. With no cushion to fall back on, the blank spaces on my calendar felt like a taunt, and every week without a booking felt like failure. There were moments when I questioned if I'd made a mistake.

But in those moments of doubt, I held onto my why. I wasn't doing this for accolades; I was building a life for my daughters and me—one built on resilience and the courage to pursue my passions. I leaned into the discomfort, learning from setbacks and adapting after failures. Slowly but surely, progress came—not as overnight success, but as steady, hard-earned growth fueled by persistence.

My first break came when I pitched myself to a local food tour group. What began as a one-time opportunity evolved into a three-year collaboration. I captured the essence of the tours—laughter, vibrant dishes, and the charm of historic buildings—while honing my craft. Around the same time, I applied for a real estate photography contract with a marketing firm, battling imposter syndrome but taking the leap anyway. To my surprise, I got the job.

The steady work refined my skills and taught me what clients valued, but it also revealed a deeper truth: Every room and home had a story, yet the firm's emphasis on efficiency and standardization stifled my creativity. Feeling boxed into a formula that left no room for artistry, I made one of the hardest decisions of my career—I walked away. Letting go of the paycheck was terrifying, but it was necessary to reclaim my vision and authenticity. It wasn't just about leaving a job; it was a declaration that I valued my creativity enough to take risks.

Looking back, those opportunities—the food tours and real estate photography—were pivotal in shaping my business and myself. They taught me to say yes, even when unsure, and to trust my instincts. They also taught me the courage to walk away from what no longer served me and the importance of believing in my ability to navigate uncertainty.

Building this business wasn't just about creating a career—it was about rediscovering who I was. For years, I had lived as the supporting figure behind others, but when my marriage ended, that identity crumbled, forcing me to confront a new question: Who am I now?

Photography became the answer. It allowed me to reclaim myself in ways I had never imagined. Through my lens, I wasn't just capturing images; I was creating a narrative, one that spoke of resilience, strength, and transformation. I was no longer the background figure—I was the creator, the artist, the businesswoman. Every frame I captured reminded me that I could take something ordinary and make it extraordinary.

As my business grew, I began connecting with women navigating their own transitions—downsizing after divorce, starting over after loss, or adjusting to an empty nest. They'd often ask how I managed to rebuild, and my answer was always the same: "I got divorced." That response surprised them, sometimes eliciting sympathy, but I didn't need it. My divorce wasn't the end of my story—it was the beginning. It transformed fear into purpose and loss into a fresh start, and sharing that truth often opened the door for them to share their own stories of resilience and hope.

What I didn't expect was how much their stories would reflect my own. These women, whom I met because of my photography, became mirrors of my journey. Their courage reminded me of my own, and their vulnerability allowed me to honor my struggles. Each connection deepened my sense of purpose, making my work feel like a mission rather than a job.

Sometimes, my sessions became moments of catharsis. I'd listen as they shared their fears and hopes, and their stories often brought tears —both theirs and mine. Other times, we laughed, finding joy in life's unexpected moments. I wasn't just a photographer; I was a witness to their transformations and a reminder that even shattered lives can be rebuilt into something beautiful.

Through these experiences, I realized my work was about more than creating beautiful images. It was about connection, healing, and celebrating resilience. Each photo became a testament to the power of rising after adversity and redefining one's life. Reclaiming myself through my work gave me a purpose greater than photography—it became a way to inspire others to see the strength in their own stories.

Looking back at the woman who closed that laptop, trembling and shattered, I see someone who didn't yet realize the strength within her. That moment of pain became the catalyst for transformation, revealing a resilience that had been waiting to rise.

I wish I could tell her she didn't need all the answers yet—that her tears would one day nurture the seeds of something remarkable. What felt like the end was really the beginning of a story she would write with courage and determination.

She didn't know then that her fear would fuel her journey or that the broken pieces of her life could be rebuilt into something entirely her own. But I know now. Every step she took, no matter how small, was an act of defiance against despair. Every time she showed up for her daughters, her clients, and herself, she proved she was capable of more than she ever dreamed.

Her journey wasn't easy—filled with heartbreak, doubt, and exhaustion—but the moments of triumph and clarity shone brighter because of the darkness that came before them. Every painful step was worth it.

Today, I know I am not defined by what happened to me but by how I responded and rebuilt. The woman who closed that laptop was scared, but she was also braver than she knew.

PROMPTS FOR REFLECTION

1. What moment in your life felt like an ending—but ultimately became a beginning? Explore a time when something you deeply relied on fell apart. What did it reveal about you? How did that moment open the door to something new, even if you couldn't see it at the time?

2. When have you stepped into a new identity after life forced you to let go of an old one? Reflect on a time when you had to rediscover yourself—after a move, a breakup, a job loss, or another major life shift. What version of yourself emerged? What did you learn about who you truly are?

3. What gifts or strengths have you discovered through pain or uncertainty—and how can you use them to support others? Think about how your journey, especially the hard parts, has shaped the person you are today. What do you now offer the world (or even one person) because of what you've lived through?

UNSTOPPABLE IS AN INSIDE JOB

SUSAN TRUMPLER

> *You may not control all the events that happen to you, but you can decide not to be reduced by them.*
>
> — MAYA ANGELOU

*I*t is a little ironic that it took me until my fifties when I finally realized I wasn't your average, run-of-the-mill woman. For most of my life, I measured myself against others. In high school, when all my friends started dating long before I did, I silently labeled myself the loser—the one left behind, the one not chosen. Later, when college SAT scores came in, mine were solid but unremarkable, nowhere near the valedictorians. Just like that, I had more "proof" that I was nothing special.

Life kept showing up with its own kind of pop quizzes—moments that seemed to measure how "successful" I was. And after each one, I adjusted my internal scale of worth. A silent tally of wins and losses, constantly shifting based on how I performed or how I felt I stacked up.

- Go to college: Check.

- Drop out before graduating: Ding.
- Get married young: Check.
- Get divorced after twenty years: Ding.
- Bring two beautiful daughters into the world: Check, check.
- Climb the corporate ladder and enjoy a comfortable lifestyle: Check, check.
- Get fired without warning: BIG FAT DING!

I'll never forget that Friday afternoon when my phone rang. It was my boss calling to say the company was downsizing and my services were no longer needed. No conversation. No compassion. Just a few cold sentences, and it was over. I sat there, stunned. I had built a career, delivered results, climbed the ladder—and just like that, I was out.

I had a choice to make. I could sit in that moment and stew in my anger, or I could figure out what came next. I was a single woman, three thousand miles from home, with a couple months' severance and no real plan. But I wasn't completely unprepared.

Earlier that year, on a hunch I couldn't quite explain, I had packed my life into storage, keeping only my work essentials, some clothes, and my car. I'd rented out my home and hit the road to explore the country—living in furnished apartments for four to six weeks at a time. As long as I had internet and airport access, I could follow my employer's remote work policy and keep moving.

And now, here I was—freed from a job I didn't leave by choice, facing a blank page in the middle of my story. Life had thrown me a curveball, and the real question became: *How was I going to handle it?* Would I let it define me or fuel me?

I remembered something a coach and mentor once told me: "Susan, no one ever said life is supposed to be easy. The sooner you accept that life is fifty percent positive and fifty percent not-so-great, the sooner you'll learn, grow, and thrive from the experiences you perceive as less than ideal."

At the time, I didn't fully understand the weight of her words. But after that layoff—and so many other moments since—I realized what she meant. Life has its rhythm. The highs feel incredible, but real growth? That happens in the valleys. In the struggle. In the silence after a door slams shut and you're left asking, *Now what?*

I'd had my share of mountaintops and lowlands. Losing my job was just one chapter. There were others—some harder, some sweeter. But with age came clarity. Wisdom. And now, as someone who's navigated a few storms, I carry a few truths close to my heart.

Those lessons weren't learned in the easy seasons. They came from getting back up after being knocked down—over and over again. And if my story can offer any encouragement, it's this:

- You are not defined by your circumstances.
- You are shaped by how you respond to them.

If you're walking through a valley now, keep going. The climb out may not be easy, but I promise—it's worth it.

LESSON 1: TAKE A BREATH—YOUR FIRST REACTION MIGHT LEAD YOU IN THE WRONG DIRECTION

One of the most transformative steps I ever took in my personal and professional growth was earning my master's certification in neuro-linguistic programming (NLP). NLP explores how we're wired for behavior—why we react the way we do and how we can shift those patterns. It helped me understand the two major systems at play in my brain: the logical, analytical side that makes reasoned decisions and the primitive, survival-focused system that's always scanning for threats.

The problem? That survival system was outdated—kind of like a sweet but nervous grandmother insisting I'd catch pneumonia if I went outside with wet hair. Well-meaning but out of step with reality.

Understanding that about myself became essential during my career crisis. When I lost my job, my primitive brain went into full-blown panic mode. It screamed that I was too old, that no one wanted my skills, that I'd end up living under a bridge with my belongings in a shopping cart. I could feel the fear rising—my fight-or-flight instincts gearing up to accept the first job that came along, no matter how ill-fitting. (Door greeter at Walmart? That one made a strong appearance.)

But I knew better. I had to hit pause.

I reminded myself that the primitive brain always moved faster than the logical one. If I didn't create space for my reasoning mind to catch up, I'd let fear drive every decision. So I took a breath—literally. I sat myself down, closed my eyes, and breathed deeply, trying to ground myself in the present instead of spiraling into worst-case scenarios.

And it wasn't easy. I had never been unemployed before. The shame felt heavy, and the fear was sharp. But I leaned on every personal development tool I had ever learned, whispering to myself, *Okay, little missy, slow it down. Step back. Let's figure out what's real—and what you're making up in your head.*

I turned to my most trusted practice: journaling.

At first, I wrote from a place of panic. *What am I going to do? How will I pay the bills? Who would even hire me now?* Not surprisingly, those questions led nowhere. The answers only reinforced fear and a narrative of scarcity.

But something shifted as I kept writing. My questions began to change. *What do I love to do? Who do I admire? Who has already benefited from my work?*

And suddenly, the answers started to flow.

I reflected on the moments in my career that had filled me up—the clients I had supported, the breakthroughs I had witnessed, the impact I had made. The fear began to loosen its grip, replaced by a quiet sense of worthiness and possibility. No genie showed up with a golden job offer, but I started making lists. Ideas came to me more easily. I thought of people I could call, opportunities I hadn't considered, and the spark of hope began to flicker again.

That shift—from fear to curiosity, from survival mode to grounded self-worth—changed everything. It didn't solve everything overnight, but it gave me a path forward. A breath. A question. A new beginning.

LESSON 2: VULNERABILITY WAS MY FRIEND (EVEN WHEN I DIDN'T WANT IT TO BE)

Just when I started to feel hopeful about my career prospects again, a new hurdle appeared—one that hit squarely at my pride. If I wanted to make real progress, I had to come clean. I had to tell people what had happened. That meant admitting to colleagues and contacts that I'd lost my job—and that thought crushed my ego.

My default in hard times had always been to withdraw. To retreat inward and figure it out on my own. I didn't want pity. I didn't want judgment. I feared being seen as anything less than capable.

For most of my life, I had built my identity around being the woman who had it all together. I was the one who took care of herself, who climbed the corporate ladder, who owned nice cars and traveled internationally. I had crafted a polished image over years of high achievement—and now, with one phone call, that carefully curated version of myself felt like it was unraveling. I didn't know who I was without it.

The truth is our identities are fragile. We live inside the stories we've told about ourselves, and when that story changes—when life cracks the shell we've built—it can feel like we're losing everything. I found myself asking: *Can I really let people see me like this? Can I be vulnerable and still be respected?* Then I asked a more powerful question: *Is it even safe **not** to?*

Because if I couldn't show up fully—failures and all—what kind of relationships did I really have? If someone wasn't willing to hold space for the 360-degree version of me, then maybe they weren't meant to be in my circle at all.

Logically, I knew most people didn't judge me nearly as harshly as I judged myself. Some of them even loved me just for being me—not the polished version, not the LinkedIn-worthy résumé, but the real, raw human underneath. But testing that theory? Terrifying.

Still, I knew I had to reach out to my network for job leads. And that meant telling the truth. Not spinning it. Not sugarcoating it. Just saying it: *I was let go.*

My first reaction? Absolutely not. I couldn't bear to say those words. I didn't want to be "that woman"—the one who got fired. I wanted to find something first, land a new role, and then casually announce it as if it had fallen into my lap like some irresistible opportunity.

But time was ticking, and I didn't have the luxury of pretending. I made the decision to be honest, to tell people what had happened and ask for help—not just because I had to, but because deep down, I wanted to stop hiding.

There's a quote I love: *"What other people think of you is none of your business."* And it's true. Suppose someone judged me for going through a layoff, that said more about their fears than mine. Most people, I realized, weren't thinking, *"Wow, what a failure"*—they were thinking, *"Thank God it wasn't me."* Some probably spiraled into their own anxiety the minute I said it.

But here's the beautiful part: When I opened up, people opened their hearts in return. I started having vulnerable conversations with people I'd built relationships with over the years, and what I saw was humanity—generosity, kindness, empathy. My honesty didn't diminish their respect for me; it deepened our connection.

And yes, I benefited. Contract work started to appear. My calendar filled. My income stabilized. But I wasn't the only one who gained something. The people I reached out to felt empowered to help. It gave them purpose, joy, and a way to give back to someone they cared about.

As women, many of us struggle to receive. We'd rather be the helper, the strong one, the giver. But through that season of my life, I discovered a truth that changed everything:

Being unstoppable isn't about holding it all together. It's not about a flawless exterior or doing everything alone. It's about having the courage to say, *"I need help."* To allow people to see the cracks. To let them love us anyway.

We picture unstoppable women as fierce warriors in Wonder Woman armor. But that's only half the truth. The rest? She's got a soft heart. One that knows how to give—and one that's finally learned how to receive. All she has to do is call it in.

LESSON 3: ASTONISHING THINGS HAPPENED WHEN I LET GO OF THE OUTCOME

Before I share this final lesson on my journey to becoming unstoppable, let me first define what that word truly meant to me. The dictionary says "unstoppable" is about relentless pursuit—a refusal to quit on goals or objectives. And yes, that had always described me well. I was relentless. Like a dog with a bone, once I latched onto an idea, I couldn't let it go.

My mom loved to tell stories about my stubborn streak. As a toddler, I had a dramatic habit of holding my breath until I nearly passed out when I didn't get my way. Her solution? She kept small vases of rosebuds around the house. When I pitched a fit, she'd calmly lift a vase, set the flowers aside, and threaten to pour the water over my head. A few cold soakings were all it took to break that particular habit—but not the will behind it.

That strong-willed nature never left me. What changed over time wasn't the intensity—it was the attachment. Where I had once clung tightly to very specific outcomes, believing my worth was tied to whether or not I hit the mark, I eventually learned that there had to be room for improvisation. Flexibility. Openness to the unexpected.

I learned that lesson—like most big ones—the hard way.

When I lost my job in my mid-fifties, I went straight into fix-it mode. My mind became a racetrack, my thoughts sprinting in one direction: *Find another job. Fast.* I made lists. I scoured job boards. I asked myself which companies were hiring, which roles I could slide into, who I knew that might be able to get me in the door. The goal was simple: replace my salary. If I actually liked the job, well, that would be a bonus. But in those early days, desperation was calling the shots.

And then, something unexpected happened.

Because I had chosen vulnerability—because I had let go of the shame and told my colleagues the truth—opportunities I hadn't even considered began to surface. Three separate contacts reached out and said something like, *"Actually … I could use some help in my business. Would you be open to some contract work?"*

I hadn't even thought about consulting. But I said yes. It felt like a stopgap—a temporary fix to keep the lights on. And that would've been enough.

But it turned out to be so much more.

By slowing down, by pausing to think logically, and by choosing to be open rather than attached to a specific outcome, I created space for something better to emerge. One of those contract gigs became a favorite. Within a year, the owner approached me and asked, "Would you ever consider buying the business?"

I hadn't dreamed of becoming an entrepreneur. That wasn't part of the plan. But the answer was yes. I became an accidental business owner.

That was fifteen years ago.

Since then, I've run that company with pride—and now, alongside my daughter, who joined me as my business partner. Together, we've even launched a second company, one that empowers women entrepreneurs to step into their own unstoppable journeys.

Of course, there were moments along the way when I questioned everything. When I fantasized about the predictable security of a paycheck and a cubicle. But whenever that old fear crept in, I remembered: That was just my primitive brain trying to protect me. It hated uncertainty. It wanted safety. But growth only happens when we're willing to stay in the discomfort and move through it.

And every single time I've done that—every time I've chosen courage over comfort—there's been something beautiful waiting on the other side.

This lesson taught me that letting go of attachment isn't about losing focus—it's about making room for possibility. Astonishing things can happen when we loosen our grip just enough to let life surprise us.

Friend, if you've seen yourself in these words, I hope you feel encouraged. And even if your journey has looked nothing like mine, I'd love to hear your story. Let's connect in the She Boss Cafe and get to know one another.

Until then, go get 'em. I'm cheering you on—because I know, deep down, you're unstoppable too.

PROMPTS FOR REFLECTION

1. When has fear tried to take the wheel in your life—and what happened when you paused instead of reacting? Reflect on a time when your initial reaction might have led you in the wrong direction. What shifted when you gave yourself space to breathe, assess, and choose differently? How might fear have been trying to protect you, and what did it teach you?

2. Where in your life are you hiding your truth—and what might become possible if you let yourself be seen? Think about the image you project to the world. Is there a gap between how others see you and how you really feel inside? What would it mean to let go of perfection and embrace vulnerability? What relationships might deepen if you did?

3. What would open up for you if you released your grip on a specific outcome? Consider a goal or desire you're holding tightly. What might happen if you softened your attachment and created space for a different (and perhaps better) result? Have there been moments when letting go led you somewhere you didn't expect—but deeply needed?

EMBRACING THE WOMAN
IN THE MIRROR

SUSAN CREWS

> *I am not free while any woman is unfree, even when her shackles are very different from my own.*

— AUDRE LORD

I had been counting down to this trip for nearly a year. Every detail was planned with the precision of a military operation—the outfits, the shoes, the coats, the gloves, the hats. And of course ... the food. Yes, you read that right. The final items packed into our suitcases for our adventure to London, England, for my thirteenth birthday, were small, four-ounce cans of peas, green beans, and tuna.

Because that's what you bring when you're a lifetime member of WeightWatchers.

I had earned that "honor" two years earlier, at just eleven years old. "Congratulations!" they said. "You're a lifetime member of WeightWatchers!" I remember smiling politely, my cheeks burning with confusion and shame. What eleven-year-old wants to tell her friends that one of her first major life milestones was dieting successfully?

Not me.

Neither my mom nor I were significantly overweight. Sure, Mom carried a few extra pounds, but I never saw her as anything other than beautiful and radiant. As for me, I was just a chubby preteen—soft around the edges, sure, but far more preoccupied with school friends and after-school snacks than with calories or body mass index. At least I should've been. However, instead, we attended meetings. We weighed in. We clapped for each other's losses like it was a victory over our own bodies.

Why? Because my dad had an aversion—a visceral, deep-seated discomfort—with anyone he perceived as overweight. I never understood the full story. Maybe he equated weight with weakness, with a lack of discipline or pride. Maybe he had his own unspoken struggles with body image or self-worth. But in our house, weight wasn't just about health. It was about control. And control, in our family, often masqueraded as love.

His words were rarely direct, but they hit hard just the same. The way his eyes lingered on my plate when I reached for seconds. The tight, silent disapproval that filled the air like smoke when I gained weight. The rare, fleeting praise when I lost it—like I'd earned a piece of affection. Approval felt like a transaction. And the currency? My size.

I wanted him to be proud of me. I wanted to be seen, celebrated, loved—unconditionally. But in our home, love was often wrapped in condition. Fit the mold. Don't take up too much space. Be disciplined. Be pleasing. Be "in control." If you couldn't manage that? Then brace yourself—for the screaming, or worse, the silence.

And so, we packed cans of peas and tuna next to birthday sweaters and walking shoes. Because even in London, even on a trip that was meant to be joyful and free, the scale still followed us.

Every Thursday night for two years, my mom and I climbed into her candy-apple-red Mustang and drove to our weekly Weight-Watchers meeting. It became our ritual—a strange kind of bonding that felt more like obligation than choice. We walked through those doors with plastered-on smiles, each of us gripping our little booklets like they were tickets to a club we never asked to join.

The moment we stepped inside, the energy shifted. The air felt heavy, thick with anticipation and quiet anxiety. Women fidgeted in their folding chairs, their eyes flickering toward the scale like it was both a confessional and a guillotine. Some whispered encouragements to one another, soft as secrets. Others stared straight ahead, trapped in their own mental math— what they'd eaten, what they hadn't, what they wished they could forget.

Then came the weigh-in. Every week, that tiny metal platform loomed like a stage I had to perform on. I'd step up, heart racing, shoulders tense. I always took a breath and held it, as if holding my breath could somehow make me weigh less—as if that final inhale might save me from the shame of gaining an ounce too many.

The meeting leader's face told me everything before she even spoke. One glance, and I knew—had I been "good"? Had I followed the plan? Had I earned praise? Or had I failed, again? And then the number came. Spoken aloud. Written down. Stamped into my booklet. Etched into my self-worth.

When I lost weight—even just half a pound—I felt the rush of relief, like I'd narrowly avoided disaster. I'd allow myself a small smile, a moment of pride. But when the number went up, the shame came down hard. I wanted to disappear. My chest burned, and my eyes searched the room to see if anyone else had noticed. Were they judging me? Or worse—pitying me?

Sitting there, a child among adults, was disorienting. I watched grown women share their battles with temptation—the slice of birthday cake they turned down, the bagel they skipped. Their wins were my wins. Their slips, my shame. I didn't fully understand what we were all chasing, but I understood this: My body was a problem that needed fixing.

That belief seeped into me, quiet and slow like a leak behind the walls. I felt it when I hesitated before reaching for food, when I celebrated the scale dipping lower, when I held my breath as the numbers were called. I didn't yet have the language for internalized shame, for disordered thinking, for a culture obsessed with shrinking. But I had the feelings. And they ran deep.

The number on the scale dictated everything. If it was down, I felt like I'd done something right. If it was up, the guilt settled in like fog, thick and hard to shake. I learned early that food wasn't just food. It was power. It was punishment. It was the thing you measured in tablespoons and regret.

Eventually, we hit our goal weight. We became Lifetime Members of WeightWatchers. That meant we had officially "made it." But what did that even mean? Had I won something? Or had I just lost something far more important—like the ability to see myself as more than a number on a scale?

At ten years old, I should have been celebrating milestones like beating my personal best in swim meets, memorizing lines for school plays, or preparing for my baptism. But instead, the achievement I was praised for—the one that earned me applause—was shrinking. I had mastered the art of restriction, of self-discipline, of making my body smaller. I remember holding that little WeightWatchers booklet in my hands, the pages stamped with numbers like medals. I was supposed to feel triumphant. But it didn't feel like victory. It felt like a trade.

I had spent so much time learning to count points, fearing "bad" foods, and riding the emotional roller coaster of a number going up or down. And now that we'd "arrived," I couldn't help but wonder— what now? Would I have to keep doing this forever? Would every bite I took always carry the weight of shame or pride? Would my worth always be measured in ounces and pounds?

I wanted to feel proud. I wanted to celebrate. But instead, I felt confused. Somewhere along the way, I had internalized the belief that my appearance—my ability to be thin—was the most important thing about me. I didn't fully understand what that belief would cost me. Not yet.

Looking back now, I see it all so clearly. Achieving Lifetime status was both a blessing and a curse. Yes, I learned things—about nutrition, discipline, and how to set and achieve goals. But I also learned things I should never have had to learn at that age—how to deny my hunger, how to tie my value to a number, how to be at war with my own body.

The blessing: I learned how to nourish my body, how to plan ahead, how to pursue a goal with focus and intention. I learned that discipline, when balanced, can be empowering. I learned how to move with purpose, how to fuel myself for energy and strength.

But the curse? It ran deeper. I learned that beauty and worth were conditional. That the mirror could be a jury. That other people's opinions about my size mattered more than my own sense of self. I learned to fear food. I learned that hunger was shameful. In college, my dad's warnings about the dreaded "Freshman Fifteen" haunted me. I skipped meals and ate hard-boiled eggs and lettuce like they were penance, believing that thinness equaled success.

For years, I struggled with body image. I perfected self-criticism like it was a second language. I couldn't eat cake, cookies, or even ice cream without a side of guilt. Into my forties, I still felt the sting of shame when I ate something I "shouldn't." Compliments about my weight loss were like gold stars on an invisible report card. They felt good—for a moment. But they also reinforced the message that my value only showed up when I disappeared a little more.

I got stuck. Caught in a cycle of shame and striving. My body became a project that was never quite finished, never quite good enough. Lose weight. Gain weight. Overeat. Don't exercise. Undereat. Overexercise. Round and round I went, on the longest ride of my life.

If there were a *Guinness World Record* for the most weight lost and gained by a single person—or for the longest emotional roller coaster —I might have won.

And the most heartbreaking part? No one knew.

On the outside, I looked like I had it together. I smiled. I performed. I showed up. But inside, I was exhausted—stuck in a cycle I didn't know how to get off of, desperate to be free from a story I hadn't written but had been living since childhood.

One Monday before Thanksgiving, my body decided for me.

It was as if years of striving, proving, and pushing to meet impossible standards had finally caught up with me. The expectation to be everything to everyone—the perfect wife, mother, businesswoman, and friend—had become too much. I had been living on fumes, running on empty, fueled by a lifelong belief that my worth was tied to achievement. Whether it was weight, work, or making everyone else happy, I had learned that love and approval came at the cost of self-sacrifice.

I didn't know how to stop. I had been conditioned since childhood to earn my value through effort. The same perfectionism that once had me counting calories now had me overscheduling, saying yes when I desperately needed to say no, and ignoring my exhaustion in the name of "being good."

That night, I set the Thanksgiving table early. I imagined the joy of family gathering together, but underneath that anticipation was a deep, unshakable exhaustion I had been ignoring for years. I had always pushed through hunger, through discomfort, through self-doubt—so why wouldn't I push through exhaustion, too?

I bent down to pull the table leaf from under the bed, and in an instant, my body gave out. I collapsed onto the floor.

It wasn't just physical fatigue—it was a full-body shutdown. The weight of it all—every unspoken expectation, every quiet self-betrayal, every moment spent proving myself—came crashing down. Lying there on the floor, unable to move, I finally saw the truth: The same belief that once tied my worth to the scale now tied it to how much I could do. My value had become conditional again—no longer based on size but on service. The people-pleaser in me had completely taken over, and somewhere along the way, I had lost myself.

That moment became the spark that ignited my healing.

I enrolled at the Institute for Integrative Nutrition, determined to understand health as something more than dieting and restriction. I pursued a Holistic Health Coach certification, eager to reframe what wellness truly meant. I learned about *bio-individuality*—the idea that there is no one-size-fits-all approach to health. I embraced the 80/20 philosophy, allowing myself to enjoy food without shame, to celebrate and nourish without guilt.

I let go of the labels—no more "good" or "bad" food. I simply ate. And for the first time in years, I felt nourished—body and soul.

Hungry to share what I was learning, I dove deeper. I earned certifications in personal training, Pilates, and water aerobics. I believed the more I knew, the better I could help myself—and other women—find balance and freedom.

But something still didn't feel right.

During a coaching session, one of my clients shared with me that she felt deprived. She was labeling food, obsessing over the scale, and caught in the same cycle I thought I had escaped. Her words landed hard. I saw myself in her. Despite all my training, I had traded one obsession for another. The rules were different, but the pressure remained.

I wasn't free. Not yet.

At the Pilates studio, I noticed the yogis—women who carried themselves with a quiet radiance. Not sculpted, not striving—just grounded. Peaceful. I was curious. I decided to try yoga—not as another workout, but as a way to reconnect with myself.

In the beginning, I still clung to what I knew. I gravitated toward power yoga—the kind that made you sweat, push, and perform. But one day, I walked into class utterly depleted. I didn't have the energy to perform. So, I didn't. I sank into child's pose and stayed there. My body exhaled. My mind went still. I let myself rest—for real.

Something shifted in that stillness. For the first time, I allowed myself to *just be*—without guilt.

I surrendered. I let go of the woman who equated worth with effort, perfection, and performance. I asked for strength not to keep pushing, but to finally soften. That day, I didn't walk out of class stronger—I walked out *lighter*. As if I'd laid down something I was never meant to carry.

Later that evening, while doing my skincare routine, I caught my reflection in the mirror. I paused. I looked into my own eyes—those same blue eyes I had criticized for years—and I whispered, "I love you."

Not because of how I looked. Not because I'd accomplished anything. Not because I had finally earned it.

Just because.

I loved the woman staring back at me for who she was—strong, resilient, radiant, enough. Tears filled my eyes. For the first time, I felt truly free.

Every woman deserves to feel that. To know that her worth is not measured by her weight, her productivity, or her performance. That her value comes from within.

I spent years chasing an ideal that was never mine to begin with. But now I knew the truth: I was radiant because I chose to love myself —just as I was. Learning to say "I love you" to myself—and to mean it —changed everything.

And it can for you, too. The more we love ourselves, the more joy, peace, success, and abundance we allow into our lives. The better we care for ourselves, the more we can care for others—not from depletion, but from overflow.

One of my favorite truths comes from Maya Angelou: "Success is liking yourself, liking what you do, and liking how you do it." And finally, I can say with my whole heart: I like myself. I like what I do. And I like how I show up in this life.

Here's to choosing self-love. Here's to redefining success. Here's to living a more meaningful, intentional, and *soul-full* life.

PROMPTS FOR REFLECTION

1. How has messages of conditional worthiness shaped the way you treat your body, your time, and yourself? Explore the early messages you received around approval, appearance, and achievement. What unspoken rules did you absorb? How have those beliefs followed you into adulthood?

2. What parts of yourself have you silenced, hidden, or reshaped to be "enough" for others—and what would it look like to reclaim those parts today? Consider the roles you've played—people-pleaser, achiever, caretaker. What did those roles cost you? What version of you is waiting to be heard and held now?

3. What does it mean to love yourself unconditionally—and what daily practices help you live into that truth? Reflect on your evolving relationships with your body, voice, and values. What does self-love look like in action? How can you nourish and honor yourself from a place of wholeness rather than striving?

THERE IS ALWAYS
SOMETHING TO LEARN

MARIANNE C. GUINEE JACKSON

> *I do not wish women to have power over men; but over themselves.*
>
> — MARY WOLLSTONECRAFT

*W*hen I reflect on what it means to become unstoppable, I find myself asking: Where does that inner fire come from? Is it something we're born with—a trait wired into our DNA? Or is it shaped over time, nurtured by experience, adversity, and the people who walk beside us? I've come to believe it's both—a mindset forged through choice, challenge, and growth.

For me, being unstoppable wasn't a natural instinct. It was something I had to earn, one step at a time. And the path wasn't straight. Life threw curveballs—some I managed to catch while others knocked me flat. But each one taught me something. Every setback carved out space for strength; every obstacle became a lesson. This was my journey—one built on fear faced, resilience earned, curiosity sparked, and the kind of strength that only grows when you keep showing up.

One of my earliest memories of responsibility came when I was about seven or eight years old. My mother, who struggled with addiction and emotional instability, worked late nights as a waitress. We lived in a tiny studio apartment with one bed. Each night, she'd stumble through the door, dump her tips onto the table, pour herself another drink, and say, "Go for it."

I separated the money into piles—one for rent, one for food, and one for whatever was left. I'd tuck the cash into envelopes and write down the totals. The next day, I'd start by recounting what was in each envelope. More often than not, the numbers didn't match. She'd taken money to buy "things," and I learned quickly not to ask questions.

What did I feel back then, at that age? It was a blur of fear, confusion, frustration—and oddly, a strange sense of pride. I knew I was making adult decisions as a child, and I didn't like it. But I didn't have the luxury of wondering whether it was fair. It just *was*. And while those moments made me resilient, they also left deep marks—trust issues, a need for control, and a fear of being wrong. In my world, mistakes carried consequences and blame, even when they weren't mine to bear.

However, those experiences also showed me something powerful: I could accomplish difficult tasks. Taking charge felt heavy, but I learned it was possible. And even then, some part of me understood—if something in my life was going to change, I had to be the one to start that change.

In my early twenties, I worked at a large bank in the department responsible for the back-end computer systems—the operating systems that kept everything running. At the time, the field was male-dominated; only about one in every hundred employees was a woman. Within two years, I'd climbed from a junior position to a senior role. I went from being someone whose decisions were only respected by my direct manager to someone whose input was valued by leaders across the bank.

The work was grueling—and at times, it felt deeply unfair. I often wondered, *Did my manager have to do all of this to get where he is?* I pulled seven-to-ten-day stretches of twelve-hour shifts with no breaks, dealt with system crashes in the middle of the night, and showed up by 8 a.m. the next morning like nothing had happened. The pressure was constant. One mistake—especially an unintentional one—could crash the entire network, and the fallout would land squarely on me.

There were nights I sat alone at my desk with a bottle of water, a few cookies, and a cold sandwich, completely drained and in tears, asking myself, *Is this ever going to be worth it?* And every time, a quiet voice inside reminded me: *I'm going to trust that it will be. I'm not a quitter.*

I wasn't fearless—I was terrified. More times than I could count, I whispered to myself, *I don't have a choice.* So, I kept going. Somewhere in the exhaustion and the constant second-guessing, I began to understand something profound: being unstoppable wasn't about the absence of fear. It was about moving forward despite it.

Looking back from the other side of fear—now *that* was satisfying.

I'll never forget the day the computer room manager walked over and said, "I've updated your swipe card. You can now access the computer room on your own—no more needing a chaperone." That moment hit me like a lightning bolt. I had earned their trust. I had earned my place.

But the day I *really* felt that deep, internal shift—that moment of *I've made it*—came a little later. One of my coworkers, someone technically on the same level as me, was in the computer room when a critical issue arose. I found out later that he had told the computer room manager, Bob, to just *wait it out.* That the system would correct itself.

Bob didn't buy it. He called my desk and said, "I need you in here right now."

I rushed in, heart pounding, scanning for whatever might be going wrong. "What's going on?" I asked.

Bob pointed to the screen and said, "Steve says to wait, and this will work itself out. What would *you* do if you were me?"

It was a defining moment. Did I go against my peer? What if I was wrong?

I asked Bob for two minutes to check something. I sat down at the terminal, pulled the logs, and did a quick assessment. Then I turned to him and said, "Nope. You can't wait. Shut it all down now and bring it back up. You'll take a ten-minute outage, but you'll make that critical deadline in thirty minutes. Wait any longer, and you won't." I held my breath as Steve rolled his eyes at me. The room went quiet.

Bob stared at me for what felt like forever. Then he said, "You heard Marianne. Take it down. Do whatever she says—she's in charge."

And just like that, he walked out.

We hit the deadline. And I learned something that day: You have to trust what you know. You have to speak with confidence, even when you're afraid. And you have to be ready to deal with the fallout—not just if you're wrong, but especially when you're right.

As my career progressed, I stepped into the emerging field of crisis management and disaster recovery. At the time, it was uncharted territory—high-stakes work that demanded knowledge, confidence, quick thinking, and the ability to pivot instantly as new information surfaced. The truth was few of us entered the field with all those skills. It was trial by fire, with most learning the ropes through mentorship and experience.

I didn't have the luxury of a mentor. Just two weeks into my new role, I was thrown headfirst into what would later be known as the Great Chicago Flood. The first forty-eight hours were pure chaos—none of us had dealt with anything like it before. We were in unfamiliar waters, making decisions on the fly, flying by the seat of our pants, and hoping we were doing enough to keep a massive federal bank running from an entirely new location.

The next fourteen days were a blur of back-to-back meetings, on-the-ground improvising, and sleepless nights. We were rerouting entire departments, securing temporary workspaces, and building out infrastructure overnight. It was supposed to be seventy-five people. Two hundred and fifty showed up. There was no time to panic. We had to figure it out—*immediately*.

It was overwhelming, exhausting, and intense. But when it was over, when the dust finally settled and the heartbeat of the operation resumed, I took a breath, smiled, and thought, *I did it. We did it.* Another notch in my "unstoppable" belt.

Sometimes, courage doesn't wait for permission. It just shows up.

I remember one night less than twenty-four hours into the disaster, I walked into an executive's office. "John," I said, "I hope it's not going to be a problem getting my expense report paid quickly."

He glanced up casually. "Why? How much are we talking?" When I told him, "A little over $100,000—and it's all on my personal American Express card," his eyes widened. His jaw dropped. "Who approved that?"

"No one," I said calmly. "You told me to do whatever it took to keep the bank running. So, I did."

He stared at me for a beat. "How much more are we talking?"

"At least another $250,000 in the next few days," I replied. "After that? No idea. But thanks in advance for getting this squared away. I've got more fires to put out."

And with that, I turned and walked out.

Courage showed up that night—because it had to. There wasn't time to overthink, no room for indecision. There was just action, instinct, and trust in what I knew had to be done.

The next fourteen days were a blur. I had an assistant assigned to me for every eight-hour shift, and I practically lived at the office. I grabbed sleep in small pockets, often on a couch or curled up in a corner. Calmness became my default mode—even when everything inside me was on high alert. I learned a lot during that time, but one lesson stood above the rest: Life will always throw you curveballs. The best way to face them is with preparation and a plan. You can't predict everything, but you can build the muscle memory to respond with clarity.

I wasn't the smartest person in the room—not by a long shot. What I did have was the ability to ask good questions, sift through chaos for clarity, trust what I knew, and take responsibility for decisions. I acted when others hesitated. I stayed grounded when things went sideways. And I learned that experience is what builds wisdom—not success alone, but the stumbles, the recoveries, and the lessons hidden in the mess.

Years later, I had a moment that crystallized all of it for me.

There was a gas leak that threatened an eight-block radius—homes, businesses, everything. I found myself once again around a table, this time with the mayor, the police chief, the fire chief, and a gas technician. Each leader called in their most trusted team members and asked the same question: *What do you know that I don't know—but need to know? Start talking.*

As the information poured in, we sorted it, made a plan, and executed fast. We minimized the risk, got the leak under control, and kept people safe. It wasn't a solo effort. It was smart leadership and seamless teamwork under pressure.

That moment revealed a truth I've carried with me ever since: Being unstoppable isn't about always having the answer. It's about having the humility to know what you don't know, the courage to ask the right people, and the confidence to make the call. It's knowing when logic needs to lead—and when emotion needs to be heard. Wisdom lives in that balance. And *that* is what makes you unstoppable.

At fifty-three, I made another terrifying decision—I left my corporate job to pursue entrepreneurship. I made a great decision to start working at my own business part-time while still holding a full-time job. Was it hard? Did I have to go out of my comfort zone? Did it take a while before I had the confidence that I would continue? Was I scared? You bet to all of it.

And, by then, I had learned that fear wasn't my enemy. It was hard and it was something I had to sit in, learn from, accept and move past. It was a sign that I was growing. And growth is what makes us unstoppable.

If I could go back and speak to that little girl sitting at the kitchen table, carefully counting coins and crumpled dollar bills while her mother drank herself to sleep, I'd tell her this: *One day, you will take control of your life. You won't just survive—you'll thrive. You'll change more lives than you can imagine. It won't be easy. You'll be frustrated, angry, scared, and exhausted—and you'll do it anyway.*

And now, all these years later, I see how far I've come. My business continues to grow, and with every client I help, I feel the deep satisfaction of knowing I'm making a real difference. In January 2025, I added a new chapter to my story: LanaLouBooks.com—a passion project born from love, loss, and a powerful desire to give back. It's living proof that we are always evolving, that our past doesn't define us, and that even the hardest beginnings can lead to something beautiful.

Becoming unstoppable was never about eliminating fear, doubt, or exhaustion. It was about trusting that no matter what came my way, I could face it. That I would figure it out. That I could pivot, rebuild, start over if I had to—and rise again.

Carpe Diem. Seize the day. And in the wise words of Spock: *Live long and prosper.*

PROMPTS FOR REFLECTION

1. Fear as Fuel: Is your fear protecting you—or preventing you? Think about something you're currently avoiding or hesitating to pursue. What role is fear playing? Is it alerting you to a real risk, or is it keeping you stuck in a place you've outgrown? What facts can you gather to help transform that fear into informed action?

2. The Power of the Pivot: Where in your life do you need to stay open to what you don't know? Reflect on a time when being open-minded changed the outcome of a decision—or when refusing to adapt made things harder. Who might have the insight or experience you need right now? What questions would you ask them if you had the courage to reach out?

3. Curiosity with Consequences: What question have you been afraid to ask—and why? Consider where you've silenced your curiosity. Was it to stay safe, to avoid conflict, or because someone taught you not to dig deeper? What doors might open if you allowed yourself to follow that question now? What would it mean to you to stop playing small and start exploring again?

BREAKING KARMA

NICOLE PADÍN CHABRIER

> *The world begins anew every time you let go of who you were and step into who you're becoming.*

— BRIANNA WIEST

I don't want to work. I want to paint."

I blinked, trying to make sense of the words that had just come out of his mouth. "Say more," I said carefully, hoping I had misunderstood.

"I don't want to work," he repeated. "I want to own my own studio and paint. That's all I want to do. It's my dream."

"Okay," I said slowly. "I support you. You can absolutely paint on nights and weekends—connect with local artists, start building your network. And once you've sold enough and built traction, then yes, go for it full time. I'm in your corner. But not working at all to support us? That doesn't work for me."

He shook his head. "It doesn't work that way for me. I need freedom. This is the only way I can paint."

My breath caught. He had worked full time as a brilliant graphic designer in Brazil for years, while also painting on the side. Why was this different?

A rush of heat surged through my body. My stomach twisted into a knot. Something in his face—a blankness, a certainty—hit me hard. My heart sank, my throat tightened, and cortisol flooded my system. Fear punched me square in the gut.

I fought to hold my composure. Where was this coming from? We'd just gotten married—one month earlier. We had spent nearly two years navigating the immigration process so he could move here and start a new life. This wasn't part of the plan. Was it his plan all along?

"I have dreams, too!" I heard myself say. Wait—did I? That voice inside me, long dormant, startled me. I hadn't even realized how much I'd buried my own desires.

But he didn't ask what my dreams were. He didn't seem to care.

"This doesn't work for me," I said, my voice trembling. "I'm not a sugar mama. This affects both of us. When it affects both of us, we talk about it. We decide together—as partners."

He looked me straight in the eye and said he wasn't looking for a "sugar mama." The words felt rehearsed like he knew the term well. But how? He'd barely spoken English until recently. The familiarity in his response sent alarm bells ringing.

Something felt off. Deeply off. And he wasn't budging.

My instincts kicked in—hard. "We need help," I said, trying to hold back tears. "I don't know how to move forward from this conversation. All I know is this doesn't work for me. We need a third party. A couple's therapist. Someone who can help us figure this out."

Inside, I was already unraveling. But I held my ground. I had to.

How had we gotten to that point so quickly? We were only a month into our marriage, and already we were talking about therapy?

There had been so many red flags along the way, but the truth was —I didn't know what to do with any of them. I had been raised to keep the peace, to avoid conflict, to never make waves or stir up drama.

I didn't have the language or the tools to work through the things that didn't make sense. So, I did what I'd always done: I noticed the red flags internally, quietly acknowledged them, and then shape-shifted. I adjusted, adapted, and kept moving forward—waiting for more clarity, more information, something that would help it all make sense.

But that? That flag—the one where he declared he wasn't going to work—stopped me cold. It was the line I couldn't cross. There was no way to work around that issue. I couldn't just keep going and hope for the best. This wasn't a yellow light; it was a full stop. We needed help. Reinforcements. Experts. Fast.

Four months later, we were sitting side by side on the therapist's couch, surrounded by the sterile calm of her office. I listened as he spoke with unwavering conviction, sharing his dream—his plan to pursue painting full time—with no regard for my feelings, no acknowledgment of how this would affect our shared life. I sat there, still stunned by his resolve, a pit in my stomach growing deeper with every word.

Something in me whispered: *Strap in. This is going to be a long ride.*

Looking back now, that whisper wasn't fear—it was wisdom. It was the first stirring of a voice I hadn't known I possessed. A voice that had lived deep inside me, waiting to be heard. Waiting for me to claim it.

I knew then that this journey wouldn't just be about our relationship. It wouldn't just be about navigating marriage or reconciling different visions for our future. This would be about me. Unpacking me. Untangling patterns I had never dared to examine. This was my second marriage, and I could no longer pretend I wasn't part of the problem.

I had a tendency—a deeply ingrained one—to fall hard and fast. Attraction and attention from someone I liked felt like gravity, pulling me in before I'd even asked the real questions: *What do you value? What do you want from your life? From partnership?* There were no foundations built on friendship, no shared blueprints. Intimacy became the short-cut, and before I knew it, I'd be knee-deep in another relationship built on assumptions and chemistry alone. Therapy would be more than a space for us to talk—it would be the place where I finally asked myself: *How did I get here? Why did I keep choosing relationships that started without clarity? What was I afraid to confront in myself?*

I was the common denominator. And that meant I had work to do.

So, there I was: married, on a therapist's couch, staring down the messy truth.

And that time, I didn't flinch. I strapped in—tight.

That one red flag—that one human—my second husband, became the catalyst for everything. The unraveling. The unpretzeling. The reckoning that would lead me back to myself. That relationship forced me to examine how I'd been conditioned, how I'd learned to contort myself to survive, and ultimately, how to begin the long journey home to who I truly was.

Early on, I realized I didn't have the language to express myself. Not really. I knew the words, sure—I had a solid vocabulary—but I didn't know how to link those words to the emotions simmering beneath the surface. I couldn't articulate what I was feeling, much less why. I didn't yet have the tools to speak the truth of my inner world.

But I saw the patterns. I watched us circle the same drains—round and round with the same hurt feelings, the same recycled arguments. I tried to speak up, to explain what I needed or how I felt, but every time I did, it triggered defensiveness and distance. As long as I stayed quiet and didn't ruffle feathers, we stayed "fine." But the moment I asserted a need or claimed a truth, it spiraled into conflict.

It felt achingly familiar. This dynamic mirrored the one I'd grown up with—where silence kept the peace and invisibility earned safety. I had learned to be the wallflower. Anything louder than a whisper invited chaos.

But this marriage took that old habit to new extremes. The stuffing, the swallowing, the burying of my true self—it was starting to eat me alive.

I was desperate for resolution. I needed to know we were rowing in the same direction. I craved assurance that we were going to be okay, that I could exhale in this relationship.

But life doesn't hand out guarantees. This was a test of patience and presence. It demanded that I slow down, that I learn to ebb and flow, to move differently. I had to rewire how I responded, build new language around my experience, and create awareness where there had only been confusion.

For most of my life, I hadn't felt seen or heard. And now, with every therapy session, I began to excavate parts of myself I didn't know how to name. I was learning how to find my voice. How to recognize my feelings. How to claim my truth.

That faint, inner voice—the one I used to ignore—whispered softly: *Hang in there. You're on the right path.*

But the deeper we went in therapy, the more he resisted. The more I uncovered, the more he dug in. And with each withdrawal, my heart cracked a little more. His lack of tenderness, his refusal to consider my feelings—it all shattered me.

I did everything I could to keep the pieces of myself glued together.

Eventually, he declared that couples therapy wasn't for him. It was *my* problem, not his. Those words hit me like déjà vu. My first husband had said the exact same thing.

Why, I wondered, was I always the only one willing to work on the relationship? Why was I the one fighting for something two people were supposed to build?

Still, I stayed in therapy. I knew I needed help navigating the wake of his choices—how to respond with grace, how to establish boundaries, how to coexist without losing myself.

And that's when something unexpected began to emerge: I started learning how to be in a relationship with *myself.*

Individual therapy helped … for a while. But I found myself looping through the same issues, circling back to the same pain. I needed more. I had been raised to value therapy—my mother believed in it and encouraged us to seek it out—but I was discovering its limitations. It helped me speak. But it didn't always help me move.

I needed something more tactile, more practical. Tools. Strategies. I needed to know where I lived inside my own self. Where I had agency. What was mine to own, and what belonged to him. I needed to know how to set boundaries, how to feel what I was feeling, how to find my way forward—not just out of the pain, but into wholeness.

That was the beginning of real healing. Not just for the marriage—but for me.

At my therapist's suggestion, I explored the idea of group therapy —something I hadn't considered before. She believed that hearing other women share their experiences might help me see my own more clearly. So I found a weekly women's therapy group nearby and signed up.

As if the Universe were conspiring to make a point, my very first group session began with a jolt of divine timing. Just as I stepped out of the train station, I saw him—my first husband. We hadn't spoken in over ten years, not since that unexpected Facebook DM where he apologized for how things ended between us. The timing was uncanny, almost too perfect. It felt like a nudge from something bigger than me, a signal that I wasn't just there to work through the relationship I was in—I was there to heal everything that came before it.

Group therapy peeled back another layer of my tightly wound pretzel. Listening to the women around me—each unraveling their own knots of grief, confusion, heartbreak, and awakening—helped loosen my own. I saw parts of myself in their stories. Patterns I hadn't yet named. Beliefs I hadn't yet challenged. It's funny how clearly we can spot other people's patterns, while remaining blind to our own.

Their stories mirrored pieces of mine and gave me language I hadn't known I needed. I realized how few of us were ever taught what "healthy" looked like in a relationship. No one had shown us how to build a strong foundation, how to set boundaries, how to feel our feelings and communicate them clearly. And yet, somehow, we were expected to just know. To just figure it out.

The more I reflected, the more the anger surfaced. I was furious that no one had taught me this life skill—that I had to trial-and-error my way through something so critical. I was in my forties, for God's sake. Why didn't I know better?

But the truth unfolded quietly. I started to see how the way I'd been raised was keeping me from living fully as an adult. My parents divorced when I was three. My father vanished after that, leaving a cavernous absence where love and guidance should have been. I didn't know what a healthy partnership looked like. I had no models. I had only ever witnessed dysfunction, imbalance, and silence. Deep down, I knew relationships had the power to shape our lives more than almost anything else. And yet I had walked blindly into them, hoping love would be enough.

After one particularly revealing group session, the therapist pulled me aside. She said she could see I was ready to go deeper. She recommended a weekend holotropic breathwork retreat—something designed to access the subconscious and unlock buried beliefs. I'd never heard of it before, but something inside me whispered yes. I didn't Google it. I didn't overthink. I simply trusted.

I drove into the North Georgia mountains, winding my way to a retreat center tucked deep in the woods. The people there had known each other for years, and yet they welcomed me as if I'd always belonged. The moment I met the facilitating therapist, something clicked. Her grounded presence, her calm energy—it gave me full-body chills. A soul-body yes. I knew, without doubt, that she was meant to be part of this next chapter.

I was ready for the next layer of my unpretzeling.

In that circle of strangers-turned-kindred spirits, I witnessed something I had never seen before: deep, unfiltered human vulnerability. Realness that floored me. There was no pretense, no performative healing, just raw truth shared without shame. I was in awe. Shocked, even. No one in my family, my friendships, or my relationships had ever modeled this kind of emotional intimacy. It left me breathless with both hope and hunger. *How do I call more of this into my life?* I wondered. *How do I find more people who live and love like this?*

And all of that came before the breathwork even started.

Holotropic breathwork, I learned, was a powerful practice. Through deep, rhythmic breathing—almost to the point of hyperventilation—you entered a dreamlike state. The music was pulsing, tribal, shamanic, and it acted as a guide through the subconscious terrain. Facilitators were there to ground us, to help us move through whatever arose, but mostly, it was us—our breath, our bodies, our memories—leading the way.

That first full day, I chose to observe. I supported another participant through her journey, needing to make sure this wasn't some cult-y experience. (Yes, that crossed my mind.) But everything about the environment felt intentional, safe, and deeply aligned. My therapist was there. The logic made sense. And that soul-body yes? Still going strong.

By the next morning, after a night of reflection and a day full of love, truth, and connection, I was ready.

I didn't yet know what would surface for me in that breathwork session. But I did know this: I was finally in the right place. Surrounded by people who welcomed truth. Held by a container strong enough to catch whatever might emerge. Rooted in a practice that honored my soul's desire to come undone … and be remade.

And I was all in.

My journey through breathwork took me to places I couldn't have anticipated—spaces within myself I hadn't known existed. None of it made logical sense, but I let go of the need to understand. I allowed whatever needed to come through to rise. Hours passed, though it felt like minutes.

Toward the end of one session, something shifted. I suddenly found myself back in my twelve-year-old body, reliving the trauma of being placed in a full-body cast after a twelve-hour spinal fusion. I was lying on a narrow, rigid strip of material as the orthopedic team wrapped plaster around me. My arms were stretched out, and I had to grip straps to keep still. The physical pain was excruciating, but the emotional pain cut even deeper.

My mother stood nearby, watching, helpless. She broke down in front of the medical team—overcome, inconsolable. They had to escort her out of the room. In that moment, I made a decision: I had to be strong. For her. I swallowed my fear, masked my pain, and wore a brave face so she wouldn't fall apart.

But during breathwork, I didn't need to hold it in.

My body remembered. My heart remembered. And as I surrendered to the memory, two people knelt beside me. They gently held my extended arms in the air—exactly as they had been during that childhood trauma. One of them was my designated support person; the other, my group therapist. Their presence was grounding, their touch reverent. They held me in that moment as if to say, *We see you now. You don't have to carry this alone anymore.*

The sobbing that erupted from me wasn't just emotional—it was ancestral. It came from a place so deep I hadn't known it existed. It was the grief of a child who had longed for comfort and never received it. It was the unraveling of decades of suppression. In their arms, I received the hugs I had needed back then—tender, human, unconditional.

The music swelled around me, guiding my breath through the waves of release. Each inhale carried strength; each exhale let go of pain. I felt as if I were being bathed in a warm, soothing balm. For the first time, I could truly breathe.

When I finally removed my blindfold, tears blurred my vision. I saw my support person still beside me, holding one hand, and my group therapist holding the other. The lead therapist stood nearby, eyes kind, fully understanding the magnitude of what had just moved through me.

It felt like I had done years of therapy in a single afternoon.

But the healing didn't stop there. In the integration circle that followed, I spoke about what I had seen, what I had felt, and how that single experience had unlocked something buried for decades. As I gave language to the pain, something in me solidified—a deeper knowing of who I was, where I had come from, and why I had struggled the way I had.

It was like I had inhaled my truest self for the first time. Speaking my truth aloud created space inside me—space I didn't know I needed until it was there.

That weekend became a pivotal breakthrough in my healing journey. It was a massive accelerant, the catalyst I hadn't known I was waiting for. I returned to the same breathwork retreat each year for three more years, each visit peeling back another layer. With every experience, I made more room inside myself. I grew more confident, more grounded, more whole.

Some people might call breathwork "woo woo"—a dismissive label for anything deemed too mystical or outside the bounds of science. But I've come to believe this: If it works, it's not woo woo. It's wisdom.

Through breathwork, I discovered a new relationship with myself. I gained clarity, emotional fluency, and a deep, embodied confidence. The inner walls I had bumped into for most of my life began to crumble. In their place, I found freedom.

My commitment to self-improvement only deepened. I was beginning to find my voice—not just in my marriage but at work and even within the complex, tangled dynamics of my family.

I joined a group called Spiritual Bootcamp, a smaller circle formed from my breathwork community. It included both my original group therapist and the breathwork therapist who had guided me through such pivotal breakthroughs. We gathered every four to six weeks to explore spiritual teachings, deepen our emotional understanding, and use meditation as a gateway to self-discovery. It was one of the few places where I felt safe enough to explore intellectually, emotionally, and spiritually—without needing to shrink or edit myself.

The deeper I went, the more I uncovered. What I found, housed in the farthest reaches of my inner world, was anger—long-suppressed and smoldering. And underneath that? Fear. Not the kind that shouts, but the quiet, persistent kind that hums beneath everything, like a low-grade static in my nervous system. I hadn't even known it was there, but once I noticed it, I couldn't *not* feel it. Fear had been driving me for years.

And it wasn't just occasional or situational. Fear had woven itself into my identity.

Looking back, I saw clearly how it had fueled so much of my life—especially the parts of me that looked, on the outside, like success. My achievements? Fear. My ambition? Fear. I had been so determined to avoid the financial instability and anxiety my mother endured, constantly wondering whether she'd be able to feed or care for us. So,

I overcompensated. I worked relentlessly. I chased security and praise like my life depended on it.

I became the achiever, the over-functioner, the people-pleaser, the one who couldn't rest until everything—and everyone—was okay. My worth became tethered to how useful I was, how well I performed, how few waves I made. I feared saying the wrong thing, doing the wrong thing, needing too much, being too much—or not enough. Always walking that tightrope.

But these realizations didn't arrive all at once. They emerged slowly, in pieces, revealed in the pages of my journal, in the stories I told aloud, in the way my body responded to certain memories. I began to recognize how fear showed up *in* me—tight shoulders, a racing heart, shallow breath. My body became a map, and fear was the ink.

The women in my family were strong—fiercely so. We didn't do emotions. We didn't indulge in softness or vulnerability. We showed up, got things done, and sacrificed our comfort for everyone else's. That was the rule. I had absorbed it like scripture: Be selfless, be useful, be perfect. Never complain. Never need.

I started to see the cost.

My voice had been stunted. I didn't know how to ask for what I needed or even identify those needs. I didn't know what healthy boundaries looked like. I found myself asking questions that should have been foundational: *Why didn't anyone teach me this? Why isn't emotional literacy a life skill we learn in school? Why are we left to figure it all out after years of pain and heartbreak?*

Fear had been steering my ship, all in the name of safety. But what I came to understand was that safety—true safety—comes from authenticity. From being able to speak your truth and still feel loved. From knowing you can show up as your whole self and not be abandoned.

So, I began teaching myself. Slowly. Tenderly. I practiced finding the words I'd never been taught. I pieced them together until they started to make sense—until they started to sound like *me*. I learned it was okay to have needs in a relationship. That it wasn't selfish or weak to ask for what I deserved. And when my husband didn't—or couldn't—meet me there, I learned to regulate my own nervous system. To hold myself. To meet those needs in other ways.

I became fascinated with the process. With how all my relationships—especially the painful ones—had been mirrors reflecting my unresolved wounds. I could finally see how my childhood narratives, my unspoken fears, and my unconscious patterns had drawn me toward unhealthy dynamics. In this marriage, I saw the truth laid bare: The undercurrent of fear that had lived inside me for so long had stunted not just my voice but my sense of worthiness.

And, finally, I reclaimed both.

I had a deep, lingering fear of losing myself—again—in another relationship. A fear of not having the right words. A fear that even if I *did* speak, I wouldn't be heard, or loved, or supported. Every time I found the courage to speak up, to express a need or emotion, I was met with a familiar wall of disregard—the same one I had run into as a child. The message was clear: I was meant to be seen, not heard.

The story I carried said it was *my* fault if someone got upset. That if I triggered a negative reaction, it meant I was to blame. I had somehow learned I was responsible for other people's emotions. So I did what I had always done—I swallowed my voice and shoved my feelings into the background.

But that containment eventually turned into rage. I felt bound, like I was straightjacketed into silence, unable to move or breathe freely. The fear I hadn't even realized I'd been living inside now revealed itself as a constant, low-humming presence in every corner of my life. And this relationship was pressing me right up against the edges of it.

My husband mirrored the emotional climate I had grown up in. And I, in turn, internalized everything—his moods, his anxiety, his silence. I made myself responsible for all of it. I shape-shifted, twisted myself into whatever shape he needed to stay calm. But the truth was, I had my own unhealthy patterns too. I micromanaged everything, trying to control the chaos around me so I could feel safe inside. But that wasn't safety—it was survival.

The people-pleasing, the perfectionism, the constant striving to prove I was good enough—it wasn't sustainable. It showed up in my body as hives, back and neck pain, sleepless nights. My nervous system lived in a state of constant high alert. Cortisol had become my closest companion.

In the quietest hours of the night, that small, persistent voice inside me grew louder. It whispered, *Get out. It's time. You've done your work. He doesn't want to do his.*

Still, I resisted. *Not yet,* I told the voice. *I owe it to myself to stay long enough to learn what I need to learn. So I never, ever end up here again.*

I dug in deeper. I gathered tools and explored new modalities. I layered healing over the bruises I didn't even know I had. And then, it happened—the moment everything shifted.

It came wrapped in what was supposed to be an apology. He turned to my mother and me and said, "I love you, but you are not my family."

Blink. Blink. *Wait—what?* "I love you, but you're not my family?" I echoed, my face flush with disbelief, my voice tight with heartbreak. WTF?

After three years of marriage? After everything we'd navigated—the sacrifices, the pain, the therapy—you still didn't see me as *family*?

Then what the hell was I doing there?

That was it. At that moment, something in me stilled. My heart stopped twisting. My body stopped contorting. My mind stopped spinning. It was as if everything in me had been waiting for that sentence to finally click all the puzzle pieces into place.

And they did. All at once. Clarity arrived like a sunrise. Calm, quiet, and undeniable. I knew exactly what I had to do.

I had always sensed these invisible walls inside me—walls that would rise up when life threw something at me I didn't know how to handle. I'd feel stuck, uncertain, small. But this time, the walls crumbled. The seas parted. And I could finally breathe.

For the first time in a long time, I felt whole.

I knew in my bones that this wasn't a marriage I could keep walking forward in. It wasn't just about him. It was about me—who I had become, what I had healed, and what I was no longer willing to tolerate. I had language. I had tools. I had strategies and self-trust. I had grown too big for the old patterns. It was time to break the soul contract and reclaim my life.

That was it. I was out. Done. No more. I wanted a divorce. That moment was the final straw.

I had done the work—deep, soul-level work. I had grown in ways that cracked me open and stitched me back together stronger. But he hadn't. At least not in the ways that could hold us together. We weren't even reading the same book, let alone on the same page. He was living his life, and I had been twisting myself into knots trying to make his life work for mine.

I had given him and our marriage everything I had. And I was finally okay with walking away from it all. No guilt. No shame. No fear. I had done my part.

Looking back, that marriage became the greatest catalyst of my life. I had to experience the pain and the heartbreak. I had to feel the soul-deep ache and that wild, ugly anger. It needed to get that hard for me to wake up to the truth of how I was conditioned and what needed to change.

It took building real awareness to see that I had played a role in every part of it. That I was part of the problem. I had to get honest enough to ask myself how I'd gotten here—why I kept choosing what hurt—and brave enough to see that this relationship was here to teach me something I was finally ready to learn.

It was, in so many ways, a rebirth.

Through the unraveling, I discovered what I truly valued. What gave me energy. What lit up my soul. I uncovered my core beliefs and motivations. I found clarity around my higher purpose and let go of the grief and pain that had kept me tethered to old stories. I picked up new tools—and a new way of being.

In the aftermath, I felt unstoppable—not because I was invincible, but because I had language. Strategies. Perspective. Compassion. I had learned how to explore, how to experiment, how to show up fully while holding myself accountable to grow. That shift widened my view of the world and deepened my self-awareness in ways I never imagined possible.

I would never have reached that point without the work. I learned how to heal myself—how to be first in a relationship with myself. I had to care for the terrain of my inner world. To understand my triggers and catch myself before the spiral. To soothe my nervous system, to calm the rage, to stop handing my pain to others to fix.

I learned how to move through fear—not bury it, not deny it, but face it head-on. I no longer saw fear as an enemy but as a teacher. I learned to listen to my body, to feel resistance, and to allow it instead of shutting it down. I permitted myself to *feel* so I could finally *release*.

That work—that deep, vulnerable, gritty work—freed me.

I became unstoppable not because I avoided hardship but because I moved *through* it. It gave me something richer than I ever imagined: a sense of peace, fulfillment, and confidence in my own skin. A deeper purpose.

The longer I lived in this Earth suit, experiencing life's heartbreaks and heart-full moments, the more compassion I had—for myself, for others, for the shared human condition. I saw how we're all conditioned to lose ourselves, to morph into versions we think are safer and more acceptable. But real healing? That starts when we choose to break those patterns, when we choose to come home to ourselves.

Being unstoppable didn't mean I stopped falling. It didn't mean I stopped crying or fearing or feeling lost sometimes. But it did mean I had agency. I knew how to face those moments, how to walk through them, and how to have difficult conversations, all while moving toward healing. It meant I trusted the process—even when it hurt. Especially when it hurt.

It took the unraveling of my second marriage to crack me open, to release the pain I'd housed in my mind, body, and spirit for decades. That heartbreak was my breakthrough. That devastation was the doorway to a new kind of freedom.

In that clarity, I saw my wings. And they were finally free to move —strong, unbound, and expansive.

Learning to love yourself is one of the most valuable skills you'll ever acquire. It's hard work. I won't sugarcoat it. But it's worth every ounce of effort. I believe—truly—that when we heal ourselves, we heal the world.

One of my favorite truths comes from the ever-wise Maya Angelou, "Success is liking yourself, liking what you do, and liking how you do it." I can say this with my whole heart: I like myself. I like what I do. And I like how I show up in this life now.

PROMPTS FOR REFLECTION

1. Where have you shape-shifted in relationships to avoid conflict or preserve connection? Reflect on moments—past or present—where you silenced your truth, shrank your needs, or over-functioned to "keep the peace." What did it cost you emotionally, physically, or spiritually? What would reclaiming your voice in those moments look like now?

2. What messages did you internalize about your worth from childhood—and how are they still influencing you today? Explore the beliefs about love, value, or safety you absorbed growing up (e.g., "I must be perfect to be accepted," "I'm responsible for others' feelings"). How have these shaped your adult relationships? Where are you ready to rewrite the narrative?

3. What does it mean for *you* to be unstoppable? Now that you've read a story of reclaiming power through healing, voice, and self-trust—define it for yourself. What would an unstoppable version of *you* look like, feel like, and sound like? What's one small way you can begin embodying that today?

AN UNSTOPPABLE JOURNEY

MICHELE SILVA-DOCKERY

 Every new beginning comes from some other beginning's end.

— SENECA THE YOUNGER

*T*he warmth of the spring sun streamed through the window behind me, gently resting on my back. I turned to look outside at my favorite tree in the backyard, its steady presence grounding me in a way I desperately needed. It was one of the small comforts that made it easier to endure a full-time job I didn't enjoy. I sat at my desk in my spacious office, trying to focus. When I looked up from my computer, my eyes landed on the nature posters I had carefully placed on my walls—an attempt to bring peace to my space. A beautiful waterfall cascaded through lush, green woods, its image meant to inspire me, to remind me that something greater lay beyond these walls.

I was grateful for the job, for the ability to provide for my two boys, but every time I thought about my reality—barely scraping by on a $19,000-a-year salary as a financial manager at a real estate agency—my throat tightened. The weight of single motherhood pressed on me constantly. I wanted to believe I could make it all work, but the math simply didn't add up.

It was a Friday afternoon, and I had just finished my tasks for the week. My mind drifted as I gazed at the waterfall poster. The image filled me with a temporary sense of calm, a brief escape from the ever-present financial worries.

Then came the knock.

My thoughts were interrupted when my boss walked in my office, smiling. He didn't wait for an invitation, just sat down across from me and, in his friendly Southern Virginia drawl, began speaking. "I've been evaluating expenses," he said casually, "and I've decided to cut overhead. Your position will be reduced to part-time in two weeks."

The words hung in the air, each one slicing through me like ice. I wondered, for a moment, if he had forgotten that I was a single mother struggling to stay afloat. But, of course, he remembered. He knew exactly what this meant for me. And still, he smiled.

I had once interpreted his mannerisms as kindness and caring. But as he sat there, delivering a blow that shattered my already fragile stability, I realized how wrong I had been. My stomach knotted. My heart pounded. I mumbled something—I don't even remember what.

When he left, the panic set in. Blood rushed to my face, and my mind spun with questions that had no immediate answers. *What am I going to do? How will I pay rent? Buy groceries? Cover the bills? Do I need a second job? Should I quit and start over?*

It felt like the rug had been pulled from under me, like everything I had fought to hold together was slipping through my fingers. The struggles of my first full year as a single mother felt heavier than ever, navigating inconsistent child support and keeping a job in an area where jobs were scarce. In that moment, it felt like everything was crumbling. But looking back, I now see that moment—that terrifying, gut-wrenching moment—was pivotal, pushing me to become unstoppable.

At home, my two precious boys—eight and eleven years old—played without a care, unaware of the storm brewing inside me. Only a year earlier, I had endured a brutal, and at times frightening, divorce

—one that left me emotionally drained and financially unstable. With no alimony, a lawyer who seemed more interested in preserving the "good old boy" network than fighting for me, and little money to my name, I had been forced to sell our marital home in Georgia. The equity I had invested was gone.

I had uprooted our lives and moved to Blacksburg, Virginia, in the hopes of starting anew. Downsizing from a four-bedroom home with a two-car garage to a small two-bedroom apartment with a den meant selling or giving away much of my own belongings. On moving day, the three of us piled up in the car with our beloved dog and cat and left for a new life in the mountains. And now, just when I thought I had found some stability, I got knocked down again.

That night, I lay in bed, my mind racing. I had two weeks.

I decided to wait until Saturday to tell my children. When I finally did, I framed it as a challenge that could turn into an opportunity. They had already seen me juggle part-time jobs to make ends meet since the separation, so they took it well. Their reaction was a reminder of their unwavering trust in me. My heart and soul over-flowed with gratitude for their love and their trust.

That weekend, as they played with friends in our apartment complex, I took long walks with Christi, our sweet, energetic dog. We wandered through the rolling hills near our apartment, the paths winding all the way to Virginia Tech's campus. The fresh air helped me think, helped me breathe.

And then, it happened.

I suddenly remembered how excited I was several years ago to get my undergraduate degree in math at the University of North Carolina at Charlotte. I then remembered the exhilaration of the day I was accepted into the master's program in mathematics education. I had felt unstoppable back then, eager and determined, before life's detours had forced me to put my education on hold.

Before heading back, I took one last look at the familiar and impressive stone buildings of the different departments. A sudden wave of nostalgia and longing washed over me.

I pictured myself inside one of those buildings, sitting in a classroom, immersed in learning once again. A spark ignited deep within me—a feeling I hadn't experienced in years. Butterflies fluttered in my stomach as I allowed myself to imagine the possibility. *Could I go back? Was it even possible?*

Excitement flickered inside me, and for the first time since my boss had dropped that bombshell, I felt hope.

Christi, sensing the shift in my energy, looked up at me with curious eyes. Not understanding the source of my excitement, she burst into a playful sprint, chasing her tail and rolling in the grass. I laughed, her joy mirroring the exhilaration bubbling inside me.

By the time we made it home, I felt both exhausted and invigorated.

That entire weekend, my mind buzzed with endless questions and ideas. The possibility of going back to school had gripped me completely, and I couldn't shake the feeling that this could be my chance. By Sunday night, I had made my decision.

On Monday, I took half a day off from work and walked into the financial office at the university, my heart pounding in anticipation. *Could I really do this? Could I restart a dream I had put on hold five years earlier?*

I had once been on the path to earning my master's degree in mathematics education, but when my ex-husband decided to move to Georgia for his career, my plans were derailed. I had tried to make the best of it, managing to land a part-time position as a math instructor at Gwinnett Tech, a community college at the time. And I had loved it. Teaching had felt natural, fulfilling, right.

But the possibility of fully stepping into that path again felt real. I was finally taking the first step toward reclaiming what I had once thought was lost.

"Can I help you?" a kind voice asked.

I swallowed my fear and explained my situation. The woman behind the desk listened, typed on her computer, consulted with a supervisor, and then looked up at me with an answer I hadn't dared to dream of.

I could apply for a federal student loan—one that covered tuition, books, and living expenses. And the best part? Credit wasn't a factor.

Was it meant to be? I had never believed in coincidences, and I wasn't about to start then. I took the paperwork home, filled it out with shaking hands, and sent it in. Within just one week, I received the exhilarating news—my application had been approved! I would receive a loan covering tuition, books, and even some living expenses. And the best part? I could start that summer. My head spun with excitement.

This was it. I took the plunge with no turning back. I knew it was a risk, and there were no guarantees, but deep in my heart, I felt an undeniable certainty—this was the right move.

With a mix of anxiety and liberation, I walked up to my boss and handed him my notice. He took it well, offering his best wishes for my new journey. But for me, this moment meant so much more. I was done with jobs that drained my soul. Done with counting the seconds until the workday ended.

I stepped into my future.

As a single mom, planning was everything. I carefully arranged my summer course schedule, ensuring it aligned with my kids' activities. The workload would be intense, but I was determined. Other parents and I coordinated playdates, taking turns watching each other's kids so we could all get things done. Their support was invaluable.

When the school year arrived, I synchronized my schedule with my children's. Mornings started with the mad dash to get them on their school buses, and then I was off to begin my own school day. Evenings were a balancing act—homework, dinner, quality time, and bedtime routines. And then, when the apartment was quiet, I sat at my desk and turned my focus to my coursework.

I was thirty-six years old, no longer in my twenties when late-night studying felt effortless. My stamina had changed, but my drive had only grown stronger. I loved most of my courses—they challenged me in ways I hadn't experienced in years. I wanted to finish as soon as possible. I wanted to build a future where I never had to live in survival mode again.

Despite my gratitude for the loan, it barely covered our needs. Every dollar was stretched as far as it could go. There were days when food insecurity became a harsh reality. I made sure my two sons never felt it, even if it meant eating less myself.

There were moments of doubt, late at night when exhaustion set in. *Had I made the right decision? Was I neglecting my boys with my heavy workload? Was I being selfish?*

Then, one night, my eldest son looked at me and said something that erased every doubt in an instant. "I'm proud of you, Mom. You're going to be an amazing teacher."

His words filled me with joy, validation, and an unshakable determination. I had to keep going. And when I received my very first A+, I wanted to jump up and down right there in class!

Being the oldest student in my program felt strange at first, but I refused to let it intimidate me. I had something my younger classmates didn't—life experience. And I had something even more valuable—an incredible adviser who saw my potential even when I doubted myself.

We spent hours discussing best practices in mathematics education, his passion for teaching contagious. Whenever I felt overwhelmed, his encouragement kept me moving forward. When fear threatened to overcome me, he inspired me to keep going.

Even now, I still have his beautifully written letter of recommendation—a reminder of the belief he had in me. A belief that, over time, I learned to have in myself. I poured myself into my studies, earning my master's degree in mathematics education at thirty-seven years old.

Against all odds.

Fast-forward twenty years to 2017. I stood in my empty high school classroom in Maryland, my desk cleared, the walls bare. It was my last day of teaching. Two decades of shaping young minds, of witnessing students grow, struggle, and succeed. I thought of the ones who had come to my wedding, the ones who had visited in their military uniforms, the ones who told me I had changed their lives.

I carried their stories with me, just as I carried the lessons of my own journey.

A year later, I discovered energy healing—a new path, a new way to serve. At sixty-four years young, I finally paid off my student loan and started my own company, dedicated to supporting others on their healing journey and transforming their lives.

Looking back, I see it all so clearly now.

That devastating day when my boss walked into my office? It wasn't the end. It was the beginning of my unstoppable journey.

And I wouldn't change a single step.

PROMPTS FOR REFLECTION

1. What moment in your life felt like the end—but turned out to be a beginning? Reflect on a time when everything seemed to be falling apart. What emotions did you experience in that moment? Looking back, how did that situation shape the person you are today? What strength did you discover that you didn't know you had?

2. When have you followed a spark of possibility—even when it didn't make logical sense? Think about a time when something within you whispered (or shouted), *"What if?"* Did you listen to it? What came next? Explore how intuition, hope, or a quiet inner knowing helped you take a leap of faith, and what changed because of it.

3. What legacy are you building through the challenges you've overcome? Whether you're parenting, mentoring, or creating something new, reflect on how your perseverance has left a mark. Who's watching you rise? How might your courage today become someone else's inspiration tomorrow?

UNSHAKABLE BELIEF

CATHY AGASAR

You gain strength, courage, and confidence by every experience in which you really stop to look fear in the face.

— ELEANOR ROOSEVELT

I have always been a competitor—not in a cutthroat way but with a quiet drive to win. Some called it a type A personality, while others referred to it as an overachiever. I called it living with purpose and positivity.

At six, I became an entrepreneur by delivering our neighborhood newsletter door-to-door for two cents per copy. I had one hundred houses on my route and loved meeting the neighbors as I handed them their mimeographed copies. When I earned two dollars for a whole route, I felt like I'd hit the jackpot.

Without realizing it, I was learning life skills: time management, relationship-building, and the basic truth that more effort often led to more reward.

The summer I turned seven, I spotted an ad for selling Christmas cards door-to-door. I couldn't pronounce "entrepreneur," but I knew I wanted in. With my parents' blessing, I sent for the card catalog and reviewed it with my dad. Each page featured a sample card and pricing info. I crafted my sales pitch, set out with my catalog, and started knocking on doors. By the time I turned nine, my passbook savings account had grown substantially.

Then, when I was ten, my world shifted. My parents moved us from our suburban Maryland home to a farm in rural Illinois. My budding business came to a halt—our nearest neighbor was my grandparents, three-quarters of a mile away. The town was over seven miles down the road, and I was limited to biking as far as my grandparents' house. For an enterprising ten-year-old, that felt like a prison.

Too young for a formal job, I did chores around the house—what my mom called "character-building"—and learned how to walk beans, pulling weeds from row after row in the fields. My parents insisted I balance work with friendships, hobbies, and school, so I waited until high school for my first real part-time job: working at a sweet shop.

The summer before fifth grade, my mom took me to see *The Sound of Music*. When I heard our high school would be performing it in the fall, I was thrilled. On the second day of school, I walked into Mrs. Wilson's English class and blurted, "I love *The Sound of Music*! I saw it this summer and can't wait to see it here!" Then I burst into "Do-Re-Mi."

That spontaneous moment became my audition. I landed the role of Gretel, the youngest cast member. I thrived during rehearsals, soaked up the applause, and felt a powerful sense of belonging. It was fun, but it also taught me discipline, teamwork, and persistence. I even pitched ad sales to local businesses for the program. Whether it was my charm or determination, I got the job done.

The following year, I returned to entrepreneurship, this time to raise funds for the marching band. I sold candy—cases of it—for new uniforms and remained a top seller for five straight years.

High school was a whirlwind of fundraising for cheerleading, the yearbook, and more. I made flyers, designed marketing materials, and did everything with the goal of excellence. I competed in everything—from academics to sports to student organizations. I was always chasing growth.

As a senior, a guest speaker at our Future Business Leaders of America meeting introduced me to the power of affirmations. I began practicing my "I Ams" daily: *I am capable. I am prepared. I am a winner.* That year, I won three state events and advanced to nationals, where I placed second in the annual report category—typed entirely on an IBM Selectric II.

That hot July day in Chicago became a turning point. I didn't make the top ten in my individual events, but I walked away with three lessons: No one hands you success, keep striving, and always envision your future.

Of course, life didn't unfold in a perfect upward arc after that. In college, I joined the business org Phi Beta Lambda, competed in events, and served in leadership roles. I gained clarity in who I wanted to be—a woman who could thrive in a male-dominated business world. I faced down condescension, challenged limitations, and taught others about leadership and marketing.

By graduation, I felt unstoppable. I had grown in my faith, landed a great job at a small company, and was ready to conquer the world. I was determined to become a CEO by the age of thirty-five.

Then came the layoff.

Not only was I a newlywed, but I hadn't seen it coming. My role didn't bring in billable hours, and the company couldn't justify my salary. I sat in my car, stunned, crying. *Am I a failure? Should I take a pay cut? Learn programming?*

Weeks later, I got a call from a former client. The CEO remembered my work and offered me a job as his assistant and marketing manager. It was a lifeline. I took it and soon advanced into a more prominent marketing role.

But the business world was rough. I saw how much power men held—and how little support women received. Time and again, I faced choices that pitted my values against professional advancement. Still, I held onto my faith and my vision.

By my mid-thirties, my goals had evolved. I was raising three kids, working as VP of Marketing at a growing company, and still dreaming of becoming a CEO. But then, another layoff came—this time from a company I'd hoped to one day run. Revenue had dipped, and cuts had to be made. I cried, mourned the job I loved, then decided to pivot.

I started my own marketing consulting firm. It made sense. I had the experience, the accolades, and the drive. But when I pitched my services to a local bank, they offered me a full-time job instead—as their VP of Marketing.

I accepted. I believed God had a plan, and in hindsight, that role was exactly where I needed to be when tragedy struck: My husband of over twenty years died suddenly in a car accident.

In the months that followed, I went numb. I did my job and took care of my kids, but I felt like a shell of myself. I couldn't imagine running a business, let alone dreaming new dreams. I was scared, stuck, and unaware of how lost I truly was.

Eventually, I found strength through faith, prayer, and the unwavering support of friends. I reached a point where I could walk away from my corporate role—no tears, no regret—just relief. I needed to be fully present for my children and rediscover who I was.

And then, an unexpected opportunity arrived in my inbox. I opened an email with a subject line that piqued my curiosity. Inside was a list of businesses for sale in my area. One listing stood out: a day spa just fifteen minutes from home.

I knew nothing about owning a holistic day spa—but I felt called. The pull was so strong I couldn't ignore it. I had no franchise behind me, no guidebook—just faith, experience, and a deep desire to be my own boss.

That decision became the next phase in my journey to becoming unstoppable. In my late forties, I didn't just find a business—I found a vocation. I got to help people discover health and vitality, and in doing so, I found my own.

Today, in my early sixties, I'm living a life I never imagined. I'm a functional practitioner, educator, speaker, and business owner. I'm constantly refining my work, giving back to my community, and pursuing new ways to inspire others. I believe in paying it forward, in lifting others up as I was lifted.

I never took a course on how to become unstoppable—my life was in the classroom. Through triumphs and trials, I learned that success isn't a destination. It's a mindset. A willingness to evolve, to trust, and to keep going, even on the hardest days.

I am the CEO of my company, yes—but more importantly, I am the master of my journey. Becoming unstoppable brought me a life of impact, purpose, and deep fulfillment. And it all began with a newsletter route, a Christmas card catalog, and the belief that I could always rise again.

I thank God every day for the strength, the opportunities, and the journey that led me here.

PROMPTS FOR REFLECTION

1. Reflect on a time when life didn't go according to plan— when you faced an unexpected shift, loss, or challenge. What helped you move through it? What lessons did you carry forward? How has that experience strengthened your resolve or redefined your purpose?

2. Consider where you are in your personal or professional journey. How would you define your version of being unstoppable today? What mindset, values, or habits help you keep moving forward—even when things are hard?

3. Whether it's a mentor, a loved one, a spiritual belief, or even a small sign like a yellow butterfly—who or what shows up for you in moments of doubt? How do those reminders reconnect you with your dreams, your strength, and your truth?

ROOTS AND WINGS

THERESA WILMOT

There are two lasting bequests we can give our children: one is roots, the other is wings.

— HODDING CARTER

I had a dream for my life, but it didn't turn out as I planned.

I sat with Chris on the porch swing at our flat in Wauwatosa, Wisconsin. We loved sitting there. Even on that chilly February day, it wasn't uncommon that we'd get some fresh air after a long day of work. We had been newly married for three months, and we loved where we lived, close to our jobs, downtown Milwaukee, our families, and friends. We grew up and had roots there. It was home.

"How was your day?" I asked Chris.

"Good." was his typical response. But that night, he had more. "Actually, I have something to talk to you about," he added.

For some reason, in that way you just know things in your gut, I braced myself for the next words.

"I was offered a promotion today to work on the Walmart team … and move to Bentonville, Arkansas."

I sat frozen, yet unable to hold back a response. "WHAT! Wait …

what?" Chris had been traveling to Bentonville frequently for his job. Because I used to work on the Walmart team—it was where we met—I knew what that could mean. I had even said to him, "You know, if they ever ask us to move to Bentonville, the answer is no, right?" But the offer was incredible. What I was feeling was not. I felt like I was free falling away from the safety of the life I had planned for, knew, and loved. A life close to my family, especially my mom, whom I was even more connected to in my twenties than I had been when I was younger. I knew at that moment that my directive to him—never moving to Arkansas—wouldn't stand. My life had taken an unplanned turn, and left me feeling sick when I should have been celebrating.

When I stood at that emotional crossroads—where fear and excitement, sorrow and joy tangled together—I picked up the phone and sobbed to my mom. Through the tears, I told her the news: He'd been promoted. It was a huge opportunity, one she recognized and celebrated. But beneath the pride, I knew she felt the shift as deeply as I did. In our family, people didn't leave Wisconsin. She and I had imagined a future side by side—me, newly married, starting a family, and her, just down the road. We'd dreamed of sharing the messy magic of motherhood together. But in classic form, she swallowed any sadness, focusing instead on what this moment made possible. That was my mom—selfless, strong, and always my fiercest cheerleader.

The next morning at the office, I tearfully shared the news with my coworker and close friend. She blinked and said, "I forgot Arkansas is even a state."

I stared at her, then burst out laughing through the tears. "Yes, me too!" With each person I told, the reality set in a little deeper—and so did the fear. Farewell dinners and going-away parties filled our calendar, each one a bittersweet reminder of the life we were leaving behind: friends, family, my job, my roots.

I remember flying to Bentonville to house-hunt, the landscape a stark contrast to our current neighborhood of aging, pricey homes. Here, rows of brand-new builds stretched across the horizon, fresh foundations laid for the influx of transplants chasing opportunities near the world's largest retailer. Touring those homes became a strange kind of adventure—walking through clean, empty rooms and picturing our new life there. *Maybe this could work,* I thought. And for the first time, it didn't feel impossible.

Three months later, our first-floor flat was packed into boxes, and a semi-truck rumbled up to haul our newlywed life down south. Chris flew ahead of me to get settled, and when I landed, he met me at the airport. I'll never forget that ride. I had one suitcase—just the essentials—while the rest of our life trailed behind in transit from Wisconsin to Arkansas.

The drive from the airport was strangely silent—inside the car and out. Unlike the familiar suburbs outside Milwaukee, this new place felt ... empty. The airport itself looked like it had been dropped in the middle of nowhere. Chris tried to lighten the mood, pointing out a llama farm we passed. But my emotions were raw, and I snapped, "Do you think I care about a llama farm?" Tears streamed down my cheeks. I was overwhelmed, scared, and homesick.

I was twenty-nine—newly married, unemployed for the first time since I was fifteen, and living in a tiny town far from everyone and everything I knew. I hadn't even known what a dry county was until we moved into one. Chris and I had thrived on city life—weekend dinners with friends, family get-togethers, and a rhythm rooted in tradition. I mourned those traditions, wondering what would become of them now. I'd call my mom in tears, and she'd gently remind me, "Traditions can change and still be beautiful. It's the people, not the place."

Those first nights in our new house felt like camping—just a few things in empty rooms, the echo of a fresh start. When the truck finally arrived, I threw myself into unpacking. Our dads came down to help and spend time with us, and for a while, it felt like a summer vacation. But then the novelty faded, and the weight of permanence settled in. And just like that, the emotional rollercoaster lurched forward again.

Memorial Day rolled around, and as I headed to the grocery store, grief blindsided me again. I passed a group of neighbors carrying potluck dishes toward a house buzzing with a backyard picnic—families laughing, kids running, dogs barking. Everything we had left behind. We had none of it. No kids. No pets. No familiar faces or beloved traditions. Just me and Chris in a place that didn't yet feel like ours. More tears.

What now? Who am I? What do I do next?

For Chris, the path was clear—he was stepping into a thrilling new role, the next chapter of his career. But for me? I was circling through grief, stuck in self-pity, unable—or unwilling—to see what I might be gaining, only what I'd left behind.

One moment stands out like a snapshot in my memory: a sunny Monday in June. My dad was visiting, helping us settle in. We'd just finished lunch on our new deck, the sun warm on our shoulders, everything deceptively peaceful. I pulled out a cigarette and lit it. I don't smoke. My dad quit the day I was born.

He watched me quietly for a beat before saying, with a slight smirk, "You're not even inhaling that thing."

"Hmph. I *am*," I shot back, and then added, "And who cares."

We laughed.

That moment—strange, out of character, and oddly tender— captured everything I was feeling: lost, restless, far from myself. But also, somehow, closer to him. A shared laugh, a rare glimpse of connection in a season when everything else felt off-kilter. Even in the heartache, there was a gift.

There would be more gifts, once I was willing to see them. I reached out to my former employer—a playbill publisher—and arranged to keep working remotely with some of their theaters. It was a lifeline, a slice of the life I'd known, back when I felt certain and grounded. Long before remote work became the norm, this connection gave me purpose. It reminded me of who I was *before* the move— and offered a bridge to the person I was slowly becoming.

That summer unfolded in a swirl of highs and lows as I tried to plant roots in unfamiliar soil. By month four, every box was unpacked, every room arranged. The novelty had worn off, and what I craved most was something that would help me feel *normal* again. And, as life so often does, it delivered—I landed a job.

It was a hat company that designed for licensed brands. I had zero experience in textiles, but I interviewed anyway—and got the offer. Suddenly, I had structure again. A reason to get dressed, show up, and contribute. I joined a fantastic team, and to my surprise, I loved learning the world of fabric and patterns. What I didn't realize at the time was that each brave step I took—saying yes to change, starting over—was building my confidence and, in turn, fueling my creativity. As fall approached, I finally felt a little more at home.

With a job checked off the list, it was time for another first: A puppy. Buck was just ten weeks old when we brought him home, and I was instantly smitten. He gave me something to focus on besides missing home—something joyful, messy, and full of love.

Then, when Buck was about six months old, we found out we were expecting our first baby. Joy and disbelief swirled together, quickly followed by that familiar ache for *home*. I missed my mom most of all. I'd imagined us sharing the journey of motherhood side by side. I'd seen her be an extraordinary grandmother to my sister's kids, and I longed for that same closeness. But in true form, my mom showed up in every way she could—frequent calls, surprise care packages, steady love that stretched across the miles.

And then, one month before my due date, I was let go from the hat company. Just like that, I was back in the unknown—jobless, pregnant, and still far from the friends and family I usually leaned on during hard transitions.

That's when a knock came at the door. It was a neighbor, also a new mom, inviting me to the neighborhood playgroup. It felt like a lifeline. I started going that week—baby still tucked safely in my belly —and was immediately welcomed. These women, caring for their little ones with grace and humor, gave me a glimpse of what was coming and reminded me that connection was possible, even here.

That playgroup became my anchor. The community I'd been missing. The tribe I didn't know I was still searching for—until I found it.

Taylor Grace Wilmot arrived on November 23—just one day after my mom flew in. This change, unlike the others, felt entirely natural. Becoming a mother wasn't just something I wanted—I quickly realized I was made for it. In those early, wobbly days, when I second-guessed everything, my mom reassured me: *You'll know how to care for this baby. Trust your instincts.* As always, she was right.

I threw myself into motherhood with the intensity of someone discovering their purpose. I tracked feedings and sleep patterns, whipped up homemade baby food, selected toys that encouraged development, read bedtime stories every night, and sang lullabies until she drifted off. We joined Rock n' Tots, had park playdates, learned to ride bikes, and made friends who became like family.

Just after Taylor's third birthday, Olivia Tess Wilmot was born on December 15. I'll never forget the moment they wheeled her into the hospital room, bundled in a red Christmas stocking. The perfect holiday gift. A dream. Not the one I had envisioned—twelve hours from the place I once called home—but one that filled me with more love than I thought possible. As I cradled my newborn and reflected on how far I'd come, I felt a wave of quiet pride. I could see the beauty of the life we had before the move *and* the strength it had taken to build something just as beautiful from scratch.

I'll always look back on those early years of motherhood with deep gratitude. I kept one foot in the professional world through freelance work, but my heart was home. I was the homeroom mom coordinator, Daisy Scout leader, and recess duty regular—if there was a sign-up sheet, my name was probably on it. I built deep friendships during that time, rooted in the shared rhythm of raising children. I didn't know then just how much those connections would come to mean. But I was about to find out—in a way I never expected.

It was a quiet Sunday morning. Chris and I had gone out the night before and skipped church—something that left me feeling a pang of guilt, like any good Catholic girl would. I was sitting at the kitchen table, coordinating an art project for the Elm Tree Elementary art auction when a call came through from a "414" area code. I didn't recognize the number, so I let it go to voicemail. When it rang a second time, then a third, I finally answered.

On the other end was my cousin, but her voice was nearly unrecognizable—shaking, hysterical, full of panic. "Theresa, your mom fell. Oh my God, Theresa, your mom fell ..." she repeated over and over.

I couldn't make sense of what she was saying. My brain clung to logic. "Can you help her up?" I kept asking.

What followed was a blur. Hanging up. Waiting. Another call—this time from my aunt. More clarity, but no comfort. They had used the AED. The ambulance had arrived, but it wasn't moving. *It's not good if it's not moving*, I heard someone say. Then, the words I still hear in my head: "I'm sorry. We've done all we can."

My knees buckled beneath me. I collapsed to the floor, sobbing. My mom—my best friend, my greatest cheerleader, the person I hated leaving the most when we moved eleven years earlier—was gone. She was only sixty-one. I was thirty-six. My girls were just six and three. And I had no idea how to find my way out of the darkness I'd fallen into. That time, my mom wasn't there to guide me back to the light. She wasn't here to help me see the beauty or remind me we could make new traditions just as meaningful as the old ones. Without her, beauty felt unreachable.

And yet, in the days that followed, small silver linings appeared through the grief. A dear friend offered to care for our dog Buck while we packed for the twelve-hour drive back to Wisconsin. Another friend checked in constantly—her messages like lifelines. Others brought meals, shared prayers, and sat with me in silence. Each gesture felt like my mom's love reaching out through the people around me.

I remembered something my mom once told me: That her love for us—me, my siblings—could never truly disappear. That it would always find a way to be with us. And there it was: In casseroles and text messages. In hugs and whispered prayers. My mom was still with me—just in a different form.

The life I hadn't planned, dreamed of, or even thought I wanted turned out to be exactly what I needed. The courage it took to walk that unexpected path gave me the strength to face the unimaginable— the loss of my mother. In the months that followed, I was able to spend precious time with my dad, sweet Olivia in tow, her giggles and joy softening the edges of our grief.

After my mom passed, the ache to return to Wisconsin grew stronger. Life felt fragile in a way it hadn't before, and I didn't want to spend another moment far from family. Three years later, Chris made that wish come true—he found a job back home. By then, the girls were in first and fourth grade, and for them, leaving Bentonville was heartbreaking. It had become their home, just as I had once left mine.

In a full-circle moment, I found myself offering them the same reassurance my mom had once given me. I reminded them they could carry their old friendships with them and still open their hearts to new ones. They struggled to believe it—just like I had—but I could offer them something I didn't have back then: proof. Proof that change can be scary and beautiful, uncomfortable and exciting—and, in time, full of belonging.

Once we settled into our new home, I faced a new decision: It was time for me to go back to work. Financially, it was necessary. Emotionally, I needed something of my own again. I had a choice—return to working for someone else or take a chance on myself. I chose the latter. I'd been nurturing the idea of my own business for years, and now felt like the right time to grow it.

So, I launched Wilmot Designs, LLC. I wanted the flexibility to stay close to the girls while still doing meaningful work. As they grew, so did the business. It wasn't always easy—but it was always worth it. With every challenge I faced, I drew from the well of confidence I'd built through years of change, uncertainty, and showing up anyway.

What I know now is that every brave step I took—every chapter I survived—built the foundation of who I am today. That confidence became the source of my creativity, which I now use to create visual solutions for my clients. I know my mom would be proud—not just of the business but of the kind of mother I've become. She taught me what it means to love fully, to show up with grace, and to hold space for transformation.

I see her legacy every day in the way I love my girls. Her voice lives on in me, cheering me on. Her lessons continue to guide me—feeding my confidence, fueling my creativity, and reminding me that life is a series of transformations to embrace, celebrate, and grow through.

One warm afternoon toward the end of the school year, I sat outside with the girls, enjoying the sunshine. A yellow butterfly fluttered nearby and settled close.

"Why do yellow butterflies remind you of Grandma, Mom?" Taylor asked.

I paused, then smiled. "Because I often see them when I'm thinking about her. They remind me of how she helped me through significant life changes. Like the butterfly, we've also undergone transformations. And like she always said, love remains, no matter where we are."

PROMPTS FOR REFLECTION

1. When have you faced an unexpected life change that challenged your sense of identity or stability? How did you respond emotionally and practically? What did you grieve—and what, if anything, did you discover about yourself through that experience?

2. What personal transformation are you most proud of—and what brave first step made it possible? Reflect on a time you said yes to something scary, uncertain, or unplanned. How did it shape who you are today? What confidence or creativity emerged because of it?

3. Who has been your greatest source of strength during times of transition, and how do you carry their legacy with you? Is there someone whose wisdom, presence, or love has helped you move through loss, change, or growth? How can you honor their influence in your life moving forward?

THAT'S JUST THE WAY IT WAS

SUE GRESHAM

When I let go of what I am, I become what I might be.

— LAO TZU

hen I walked into the office that day in May 1995, something felt different. It was too quiet and dark. That's when I realized I was alone. Where was Tom? Soon Joel, our vice president, walked in, his eyes scanning the room, clearly searching for my father-in-law too.

"Maybe he went to the bank," Joel said.

"If he did, he should be back by now," I replied.

At 3:00 p.m., our employees began arriving for the monthly company meeting. Some were standing around talking. Others went about their business, putting away tools or gathering items from the stockroom for the next day. What they didn't know was that there wasn't going to be a next day.

By 3:15, Tom still hadn't returned. There was no time to worry. I looked at Joel, nodded, and began the meeting. I don't remember exactly what I said. I just remember being the young daughter-in-law, the only woman in the company, standing in front of twenty long-term employees, explaining that we were shutting down the company effective immediately. As I gathered their keys and handed out their last paychecks, I thanked each of them. I hugged a few. Some asked where Tom was. Others didn't. They knew how hard this meeting would have been for him.

I said goodbye to Joel and waited for the banker, who arrived at precisely 3:45. He helped me load a few boxes of pictures and personal things into my car. Fifteen minutes later, with our office and truck keys in his hands, the banker locked the door. And that was that.

That wasn't the first time I was thrust into something I wasn't sure I could handle. Thinking back now, I remember a lot of things from when I was eight years old, living in Oak Park, Illinois, with my newly divorced mom and little sister. I remember the weekly trips to the laundromat. You wouldn't think they'd be memorable, but they were.

The three of us would walk the three blocks to the laundromat. Mom would load the washers, start them, and leave. My sister and I stayed with the laundry, playing games or reading. When the wash cycles were done, we transferred the clothes to the dryers. Mom would return just as the dryers finished, almost like clockwork. We never knew where she went. We never asked. That was just the way it was.

During those years, we went to a babysitter's house after school. We'd stay until it was time for her family to eat dinner. Then we'd walk the five blocks home alone, no matter the weather. Even in the dark. My little sister and I would let ourselves into the apartment and wait for Mom to come home, or for another babysitter to arrive.

When I was about ten years old, our evening sitter lit the gas oven, and there was a huge *POOF* followed by flames. Her hand was burned and her hair singed. I ran to a downstairs neighbor for help. The police and fire department came. I'll never forget the smell of her burned hair.

That was the last time we had that sitter. I don't think we had many evening sitters after that. We didn't need them. We just took care of ourselves.

I heard, "You're such a great little helper" a lot growing up. That's what I was. It made me feel important. And needed. And, as I realized years later, it made me feel in control.

When I got older, I learned that the State of Illinois had paid for our after-school care and that the burned babysitter had only been a few years older than I was.

That was just the way it was.

It seems I've always taken care of people and things. I've always been a "great little helper."

When I was eleven, my dad remarried. My stepmom had four kids. With my sister and me, there were six of us. I was now the third oldest and the oldest girl, which meant I was the designated family babysitter, especially on vacations. I was always partnered with my youngest stepbrother, four years younger than me. We sat next to each other on rides, in the car, in restaurants, everywhere.

The real kicker was on my last vacation with the family during high school. I had two suitcases to pack: his and mine. Our parents were too busy. I was a mini-mom, responsible for both of us. The world felt so unfair back then.

That was just the way it was.

Sue the doer got her first paycheck at fifteen working for a small dry cleaner. The owner trusted me to close up the store. It seems wild now to think a fifteen-year-old had her own set of keys to a business.

In high school, I was an average flutist. I couldn't afford lessons from the best teacher in the area, so I bartered. In exchange for lessons, I scheduled his students, made follow-up calls, and did other small tasks.

Sue the doer continued this pattern for the next forty years, always stepping up, taking control when others wouldn't. I was the soccer mom, the U6 coach, the registration coordinator, the board member, the liaison to the Park and Recreation Committee. I went from volunteer to volunteer coordinator of a 2,000-person event.

At work, it was the same. After we closed our business in 1995, I was hired as customer service manager at a manufacturing firm. Somehow, that position evolved into project management—and not just any project. I was in charge of a major software conversion. It was both exhilarating and terrifying. I remember many sleepless nights filled with doubt.

During one of those nights in 1997, I called my dad. We were close. I often said I was my father's son, not literally, but because we bonded over sports. We'd watch games together all the time. For my birthday each year, until I got married, he'd take me to a baseball game and dinner. Having a July birthday meant one of the Chicago teams was always in town. We didn't care which.

One of the best days of my life was in 2020 when I returned the favor and took my ninety-two-year-old dad to a spring training game in Sarasota, Florida—on his ninety-second birthday, February 29. It was a perfect day.

That night in 1997, I told him about my fears. He reminded me of everything I'd done and survived. He brought up the time I was thirteen, explaining to a judge why my sister and I should live with him and my stepmother. He reminded me of closing the business, selling two homes, and building a two-family house for our entire family while keeping our young children's lives steady.

That conversation has stayed with me. It helped me realize things I hadn't seen in myself. It also gave me a framework I now use with my own children. My father was being my cheerleader. It's a role I've since played many times for my family, friends, and clients.

There's a fine line between being a cheerleader and being a doer. Sue the doer takes charge and gets it done. Sue the cheerleader stands back and supports, letting others be their own doers.

That's what I remind myself now, watching my adult children and young grandchildren find their way. I often tell myself, "Sue the doer might want to sit this one out."

In September 2008, my world crashed. My boss called me in and let me go. I'd been there ten years. I expected to retire from that job. It was sudden, unexpected, devastating. Worse still, the Great Recession had just begun. Unemployment was at 10 percent.

They say when one door closes, another opens. Mine was more like the giant wooden door in the Emerald City. It took some hard knocks, but when it finally opened, a whole new world was waiting.

I didn't just lose a job in 2008. I lost a work family, my routine, my identity. Looking back, I know I put too much of myself into that job. Maybe I should have realized it when I took a conference call with our China facility at 10:00 p.m. on New Year's Eve. That year, we had a house full of relatives celebrating my daughter's wedding. That should have been my sign.

The first few months of unemployment were brutal. One afternoon, my best friend Nancy dragged me to the mall. While she was shopping, I broke down. I started sobbing uncontrollably in the middle of Boston Store. Nancy grabbed my phone and told me to call my doctor. The receptionist asked if I was going to harm myself. I wasn't. But I realized in that moment I needed help. For the first time, I couldn't fix it on my own.

Later, my husband told me he came home for lunch every day during that time just to check on me. He was scared. That's why Nancy got me out that day. He asked her to.

The second time I realized I needed help was when I hired a career coach in early 2009. She helped me rebuild my confidence. With her guidance, I started to think more about what *I* wanted.

Eventually, Sue the doer came back. I sprang into action to rejoin the workforce, whatever that might look like. I found a new family in my fellow job seekers. I discovered a world beyond the nine-to-six grind. I volunteered, took classes, and networked.

One day in spring 2009, I attended a jobseeker workshop alone. I'd never done anything like that solo. That day changed everything. I created a LinkedIn account after hearing a dynamic speaker. Then I met a motivational coach who invited a handful of us to join a group program. We had to submit our numbers to be considered. I didn't have a business card, so I scribbled mine on a piece of paper. He later told me that's why he picked me.

That was the third time in less than a year that I reached out for help. And it felt good. I didn't have to have all the answers. I didn't have to fix everything. Just myself.

During one session, the coach asked us to write, "On this date (xxx), I will be gainfully employed." I picked October 1, 2009. I had no idea why.

In early September, I figured it out. I wanted to start my own coaching business. I filed for my LLC on September 19, the one-year anniversary of my termination. I was back in control. Of what, I wasn't sure yet. I just knew Sue the doer had returned.

On October 1, I started my first online class to become a social media strategist. Since then, I've spent fifteen years as a LinkedIn strategist, coach, trainer, and speaker. I can proudly say: expert.

Running your own business is a different kind of challenge. There are sleepless nights, sometimes about money, often about new ideas. But I've been blessed to create a schedule that let me care for my grandchildren, volunteer, and serve on boards.

Most of all, I've been blessed to make a difference—for my clients and in my world.

Looking back, I see the thread: resilience, responsibility, and sense of self. I used to think being responsible meant fixing everything, especially when no one else would. Now I know that responsibility doesn't mean it's all mine to carry.

Sometimes, I say, "Not my monkeys, not my circus," to remind myself I get to choose whether to be Sue the doer or Sue the cheerleader.

As someone who had always put others first, I learned the hard way that I also needed to put on my own oxygen mask. I'm still learning that. But when Sue the doer starts to get restless, I can say, "Not now. You don't have to be in control anymore."

That's just the way it was.

And now, it doesn't have to be.

PROMPTS FOR REFLECTION

1. In what ways have you taken on the role of a "doer" in your own life, and how has that shaped your sense of identity and responsibility?

2. Sue's story highlights the power of asking for help. When in your life have you had to shift from doing it all yourself to reaching out for support, and what did that reveal to you?

3. How has your definition of resilience evolved over time, and what experiences have helped you recognize your own inner strength?

CHOOSING FREEDOM OVER FEAR

JENNIE JOLLY

 It's never over 'til it's over. You were born to be unstoppable.

— CHRISTINE CAINE

At the ripe old age of five, when my mom told me about starting kindergarten, I told her I didn't want to go—because I didn't know how to read and write. Even back then, my young soul was uncomfortable being unprepared. She gently explained it wasn't necessary to know how to do those things yet; I don't know if that made me feel any better or not. Probably not.

Looking back, I see how this moment foreshadowed some of what unfolded in my life—fear of failure, being a perfectionist, and wanting to make everyone happy. What a trifecta of things that can hold you back!

But on the flip side, more life experience has shown me I'm compassionate and big-hearted, have a helpful spirit, and am always willing to lend a hand. And I'm crazy … about chickens.

I was the youngest, the only girl with two older brothers. When I was nine, our parents divorced. I found out when I accidentally overheard my grandmother sharing the news on a phone call.

Back then, phones were attached to walls, which didn't allow for much privacy.

It was devastating, but I didn't act out negatively. Instead, I was the good girl who longed for and sought after positive affirmation. Other kids didn't see it as being "good," though, and called me things like *"teacher's pet," "Goody Two-shoes," and "brownnose."* This was the beginning of me losing my voice and downplaying my gifts and talents.

In eighth grade, I vividly remember going so far as to actually misspell a word (on purpose), guaranteeing someone else would win the school-wide spelling bee, and I wouldn't have to endure more derogatory comments. That's saying a lot as someone who loves words and spelling and worked hard to be a straight-A student.

During high school, besides taking extracurriculars like French, drama, and home economics, I signed up for a print shop class. The prospect of being the sole girl in a class intrigued me, given my teenage boy-crazy nature. But then, I actually enjoyed it. Since there weren't many females in that trade, it basically assured me I'd have a leg up on getting hired because affirmative action agendas in the late '70s had employers competing to hire women and minorities.

My plan had always been to go to college. But as a senior in high school, when a company that made dental chairs offered me a full-time job working in their print shop, I jumped at the chance. Getting paid while earning school credits sounded like a great idea, and night school provided the opportunity to finish the last two credits I needed to graduate.

I regret missing out on all the senior antics with my classmates, but I still took part in the cap and gown ceremony and had a graduation party. I decided college could wait since I already had a career and was making a decent income.

After several more jobs in the printing industry, I dated and agreed to marry someone who, as it turned out, didn't have my best interests at heart. I wanted to call off the wedding, but in my youthful ignorance, I felt like it was less embarrassing to get a divorce after six months than to tell everyone it was a huge mistake.

Six months later found me expecting our first daughter, and two years later brought our second daughter. It wasn't a happy marriage, my voice was pretty much nonexistent by then, and I was barely hanging on. But one night, I truly feared for my life. The next morning, I got up, took the girls and some of their clothes, and asked my mom if we could stay with her.

Eventually, the divorce was finalized, and life continued with me as a single mom, fraught with challenges, exhaustion, and stress. I wanted to be the person caring for my girls, but since bills had to be paid, I sadly handed them over to a babysitter.

The position I took had a predatory boss who specifically hired single moms. He felt he could take advantage of the situation, knowing that we were somewhat desperate and needed a job. It was like taking one step forward and two steps back.

My thoughts convinced me that no one would ever want to marry a divorced person with two children. But then I met a guy who had already enlisted in the Navy, and he was willing to take on an instant family. I thought I was much more mature and knew what I was doing that time around. As life would have it, we added a baby boy to our motley crew almost nine months to the day after our wedding.

Moving hundreds of miles away from the hands-on support of family and friends was a challenge all its own. Not knowing anyone or the area we lived in became the norm. Our active-duty military lifestyle led to frequent moves and frequent job changes.

Twenty-three. That's how many companies have had me on their payroll. If you include direct sales, the number becomes twenty-seven. The average American changes jobs twelve times in their lifetime, according to Zippia.[1] Always the "extra" girl, I guess I had to double down on that number.

Being *extra*verted is another personality trait. Extra meant doing more of what I was good at. And that was ok until it crossed over into giving more and more of what I excelled at—24/7—without receiving much in return. Then it became a problem. A problem I didn't recognize soon enough.

I thrived on being a helper. On being the assistant who had everything ready for you before you even asked me for it. That drive to always be one step ahead was a blessing and a curse. I anticipated problems before they existed, created solutions before anyone else noticed the cracks, and delivered results. But what did I get in return? More work. Always more work.

There's something intoxicating about being the go-to person. But it comes at a cost. I learned that being "one step ahead" didn't mean I was moving forward—it just meant I was clearing the path for someone else to step in and take the credit!

Being "extra" without boundaries doesn't earn you respect—it earns you a heavier burden. My competence, instead of being rewarded or recognized, often made me an easy target for exploitation.

If I kept saying "yes" and handled what others couldn't (or wouldn't), I thought I'd earn my seat at the table. Instead, I was stuck *being the table*—always carrying the weight of everyone else's responsibilities.

As a people-pleaser, if there was a club, I'd have been the one to start it and then compete with all the other people-pleasers over who could do it best. But let's be honest—this is something many women struggle with, especially in business.

For me, it was mostly about being indispensable. I wanted to be the one who saved the day, who solved the problems, who you could count on no matter what. But here's the thing: Being indispensable isn't the same thing as being irreplaceable. When you give endlessly without expectations or boundaries, you teach people to take without limits. Now add in a big helping of perfectionism. I thrived in detail-oriented jobs. But the dark side of being perfect feeds into over-thinking and never doing. I did a lot of that, too.

After twenty years of military life—with multiple moves and multiple jobs—our marriage ended. Those days became a wilderness time of struggle and hard-to-control anxiety. My precious mom was in the early stages of dementia, and I was trying to do everything I could to help her stay independent. Then my dream of a long-term job with a long-established local manufacturer was shattered after less than two years when they closed the plant and moved operations to Mexico.

I bounced back, found a new employer, and bought a house. Only to hear the words three months later, "This just isn't a good fit." I didn't just lose a job, but also lost my roommate, who got married and moved out. Being unemployed for six months with endless job applications, multiple interviews, and a string of "You're great, but we're going with someone else" will make you doubt your worth.

But you know what? I made it. I didn't give up, thanks to the unwavering support from my faith, my family, and my friends. With a renewed awareness of my finite lifespan, I stopped chasing things that didn't benefit me.

After so much time living in the valley of dry bones—being used and abused and sucked dry—it was time to find new ground and plant myself where I could flourish and find refreshing and renewal in a new season. I needed to learn from my past and set my sights on a better future.

For years, I resisted starting my own business because I couldn't guarantee myself an income, health insurance, or a 401k. My negative mindset came into play when instead of seeing that I could become wildly successful, I lived in fear that I'd fail and be bankrupt.

In the past year and a half (a.k.a. late in life!), I've learned a lot about my thought life because a coach (and good friend) strongly suggested I read Carol Dweck's book *Mindset: The New Psychology of Success*. Those who care about you and want to see you succeed will push you to see things about yourself that you can't, and I'm so thankful she did.

Your thoughts are like a train ... they're going to take you somewhere. Fixed mindset thoughts try to keep us safe and small, but in the end, they frequently hold us back from pursuing our dreams. Dweck recommends naming your fixed mindset persona. After some thought, I named her "Vera" because she always tries to get me to "veer a-way" from doing hard things.

My wise mom always dropped pearls of wisdom, so my brother nicknamed her "Betty Cliché." One of my favorites is, "You bring about what you think about." It's true because every action begins with a thought.

I found learning about embracing a growth mindset and believing that abilities can be developed eye-opening, to say the least. Having lived my entire life with a fixed one led me to believe, "This is just the way I am." If something was hard, I quit and moved on to the next thing, thinking that if it didn't come easily, I wasn't supposed to do it.

This flawed way of thinking left me with a trail of half-done courses. Now, I'm going back and finishing the ones that really interest me with the realization that I can do hard things, and I push through the tough parts instead of giving up.

Here are a few more obstacles that may be lurking around in your head, trying to derail your plans:

Procrastination. Ask yourself why you're delaying (you're scared, it's hard, etc.). Procrastination is a "favorite" of mine. I'm a frequent flyer. In case you're wondering, yes, I procrastinated writing this chapter! But I kept writing and, little by little, got it done.

Self-sabotage. What are you afraid of (failure or possibly even success, think you're too old to change or learn something new)? Instead of saying, "I can't because (fill in the blank)" ask, "How can I?" Having a negative thought? Flip it by adding the word "yet." "This is hard. I can't do it ... *yet.*"

Analysis paralysis. Overthinking and never doing. Just start doing the thing, whatever it is! Another piece of wisdom that got me to take action is, "A ship that's moving is easier to steer than one that's dead in the water." Nothing changes if nothing changes. You can always make little adjustments to your course ... if you're moving. Dead things don't move!

 If you're not getting the results that you want ... check with your excuses, they have the answers.

— *AISHA R. H-JONES*

Rewiring your brain takes time. And repetition. And did I mention repetition? Be a problem solver and figure out what's holding you back. Be responsible for yourself and show up for yourself every day (or at least most days!).

I used to feel like something was terribly wrong with me when I'd try to do what seemed to work for "everyone else" but didn't work for me, like getting up at 5:00 a.m. to seize the day. Ummm, no. When I found out my brain processes things differently, it was a total game-changer. My way of doing things isn't wrong. What a relief! Now, I create systems that work for *me*, not the other way around.

My thoughts used to be steeped in lack, but the abundance in my life proved otherwise. Instead of getting sidetracked by the few things I don't have, I now focus on appreciating the beautiful excess in every area of my life.

That includes my amazing husband of seven years, Chris; our cozy log cabin in the country (with chickens!), three wonderful adult children, and two adorable granddaughters! It's time for your thoughts to line up with your reality, too!

By 2021, I'd had enough of corporate life after forty-three years in the workplace. I wanted to spend my time doing what I was good at (and passionate about). So, I evaluated myself, prayed, and launched my business. I took back my power and found my voice—gone are the days when life happens "to" me. And now, as an editor, I'm helping others find their voice, too.

More than just cute, my chicken business logo has a deeper meaning. It was a conscious choice, constantly reminding me of my two-decade hesitation (chickening out!) in starting my own business. Every time I see it, I'm emboldened to keep going and keep growing.

Sure, there are days I question my decision when things don't go the way I expected. But then I'll get a call asking if "Mimi" can pick up her sick granddaughter from school and take care of her. I have the extra time to make sure my chickens are warm in the winter and cool in the summer. And I can make appointments in the middle of the day without using personal time or sick leave!

Now, instead of a thirty-minute one-way commute into town, I have a sixty-second commute to my home office. I'm happy and fulfilled editing books and writing my *Fowl Language* newsletter; it's my life's work. I have zero doubt I made the right choice.

There's only one me. And there's only one you. Follow your passion. Don't worry if no one else is doing it, because that's the perfect reason you should be. The world needs you to do and say the things that only you can. We need you to be your own kind of unstoppable!

PROMPTS FOR REFLECTION

1. Where have you dimmed your light to make others more comfortable? Reflect on a time when you downplayed your talents, voice, or success to avoid criticism or fit in. What impact did that have on you? How might you reclaim or celebrate those parts of yourself now?

2. What is one fear that has held you back—and what would change if you moved through it with curiosity instead of perfection? Whether it's the fear of failure, being judged, or not being "ready," explore how this fear has shaped your choices. What might be possible if you gave yourself permission to learn, evolve, and try again?

3. In what ways have your setbacks been setup moments for something greater? Trace a few of the unexpected turns in your journey. Where did life redirect you for the better? How did past challenges reveal your resilience or lead you to a more aligned path?

ENDNOTES

1. "Average Number of Jobs in a Lifetime [2023]: How Many Jobs Does the Average Person Have." Zippia, June 28, 2023. https://www.zippia.com/advice/average-number-jobs-in-lifetime/.

ABOUT THE AUTHORS

Cathy Agasar, author of *The Gift of Loss*, is a national board-certified colon hydrotherapist and I-ACT certified colon hydrotherapy instructor. Her own wellness journey brought her to a new level of understanding of the mind/body/spirit connection and a passion to educate the public about gut health and cleansing. Cathy and her husband, Jerry, reside and work in historic Bucks County, Pennsylvania, where they have merged their practices to serve the community together. She is the mother of six children and two cats and enjoys taking long walks, biking, reading, but, most of all, spending time with loved ones. She is a woman of strong faith, grateful every day for the life she is living, and extremely honored to share her journey with all who will listen. Learn more at https://agasarfamilywellcare.com/.

Nicole Padín Chabrier is a debut author, educational change-maker, and transformational coach whose own healing journey fuels her mission to reimagine what—and how—we teach. After breaking free from generational patterns and the pressure to please, Nicole traded corporate burnout for soul-deep purpose. She now empowers educators and changemakers to integrate emotional intelligence, financial literacy, and real-life skills into classrooms, creating a generation prepared to thrive. A breathwork advocate and practical magic-maker, Nicole is living proof that true power comes from within—and that it's never too late to rewrite your story.

Susan Crews is a heart-centered wellness mentor, speaker, and founder of The Radiant Soul Sisters community. After years of burnout from entrepreneurial hustle, she discovered that self-care isn't selfish—it's essential. Now, she empowers midlife women to break free from exhaustion and reconnect with their vibrant, radiant selves. Susan loves spending time outdoors, cold plunging, playing with her grandkids, and creating nourishing meals. Listen to her podcast or learn more at www.susancrews.com.

Michele Silva-Dockery releases energetic blockages and limiting beliefs that empower others to get their lives back, physically and emotionally. She is a Reiki master teacher and energy healer, having spent a long career as a public school math teacher. She lives with her soulmate, Dan, and her two beloved cats in Maryland, USA. She loves to be of service to others and has recently been called "The Soul Awakener" by one of her clients. Learn more at https://caringonward.com.

Anna Garrison is a photographer with a knack for capturing the soul of a space and inviting viewers to imagine themselves inside the story it tells. After twenty-three years as a military spouse and eighteen moves, her life took an unexpected turn with a divorce that became her creative awakening. What began as a personal escape behind the lens evolved into a thriving career, with her work featured in books and magazines. When she's not chasing golden light or styling interiors, Anna is likely on a solo road trip, swapping stories over bourbon, or reminiscing about frog princes—yes, there's a story there. Learn more at https://annagarrison.com/.

Sue Gresham believes that everyone has unique gifts to share and an incredible story to tell. After helping close her family's business, navigating multiple career pivots, overcoming cancer, and learning to release her lifelong role as the perpetual "doer," Sue understands resilience on a deep, personal level. Today, she's a business owner once again, coaching entrepreneurs, service providers, and everyday experts to show up authentically, build visibility, and become unforgettable on LinkedIn. Learn more at www.sue-gresham.com.

Marianne Guinee Jackson knows that sometimes the things we try don't work—until they do. After thirty-five years of working in corporate and public service, as well as side gigs, she found her vehicle for success and freedom. She continues to guide others in achieving that same wellness and overall freedom most people seek. Thirteen years later, she continues to change lives and recently launched *LanaLouBooks.com*, a creative venture inspired by her beloved therapy dog. Through coloring, journaling, and puzzling, her books support cancer research and animal rescues—and prove that purpose fuels unstoppable impact. Learn more at simplymarianne.com.

Jennie Jolly is a lifelong word aficionado and escapee from corporate bureaucracy. After years of hopping around (both states and jobs), she now crafts editorial magic, intertwining passion with profession. When she's not polishing paragraphs and policing punctuation, Jennie's likely hanging out with her family or living the fast life at a Blue Angels air show. Her snarky *Fowl Language* newsletter combines her love of grammar, chickens, and humor. See what's clucking at www.jenniejolly.com.

Susan Trumpler, the founder of Unstoppable Women in Business, is an international speaker, coach, podcaster, and author of the Amazon bestseller *OH SH*T! I'm in Sales?: An Entrepreneur's Guide to Making Sales Your BFF*. Susan expertly guides small business owners to become masterful communicators and bold, confident promoters of their brand brilliance. Join her in the She Boss Cafe to get the inside scoop on how to grow your audience, nurture relationships, and expand your client base! Visit her at http://shebosscafe.com.

Theresa Wilmot is the founder of Wilmot Designs, a creative studio dedicated to helping small business owners elevate their brand through strategic, impactful design. After returning to her Midwestern roots, Theresa faced a pivotal choice: take a job at a design firm or build something of her own while staying close to her growing daughters. She chose entrepreneurship—and never looked back. Today, Wilmot Designs blends Theresa's eye for clean, effective branding with her deep understanding of storytelling, positioning clients as the go-to experts in their fields. Learn more at www.wilmotdesigns.com.

COPYRIGHT DETAILS

JOIN HANDS WITH WOMEN WHO GET IT

She Boss Café is your virtual community of *Unstoppable Women*

Big dreams need strong support! That's why we created She Boss Café: a place for ambitious, heart-led women in business to grow together:

GENUINE CONNECTIONS
Monthly networking events and 1:1 matchups that help you meet the right people

GROWTH OPPORTUNITIES
Training and resources that expand your mindset and your business

ACCOUNTABILITY + ENCOURAGEMENT
A supportive crew that keeps you moving forward (even on the hard days)

Join us today! SheBossCafe.com
We can't wait to welcome you!

Here's to Becoming Unstoppable!

Susan Trumpler

Founder, Unstoppable Women in Business
uwibusiness.com

ABOUT THE PUBLISHER

 Founded in 2019, Highlander Press is a vibrant, mid-sized publishing house dedicated to transforming the world through the power of words. We are deeply committed to diversity and bringing big ideas to the forefront. At Highlander Press, we help authors navigate the journey from initial concept through writing, editing, and publishing, culminating in the release of a book that not only fulfills a lifelong dream but also solidifies their expertise and boosts their confidence.

Our unique approach centers on forging strong, collaborative relationships with women-owned businesses across the publishing spectrum, including graphic design, marketing, launching, copyright management, and publicity. We believe in the power of community and operate by the mantra, "a rising tide lifts all boats." This philosophy not only enhances our business model but also ensures that our authors receive unparalleled support and opportunities to succeed.

Join us in making a mark in the literary world, where your voice is heard, and your message has the power to change lives.

facebook.com/highlanderpress
instagram.com/highlanderpress
tiktok.com/highlanderpress
linkedin.com/company/highlander-press

ALSO FROM HIGHLANDER PRESS

ANTHOLOGIES

The Author's Toolkit: Mastering the Art of Author Visibility
Heart-Centered Marketing: Proven Strategies that Naturally Attract and Nurture Clients
Your First Year: What I Wish I'd Known

BESTSELLING BOOKS

Line Magic by Kris Faatz
Shelf Life: A Field Guide to Long-Term Author Success by Deborah Kevin, MA
Sometimes I Think I Suck by Tal Fagin
In Motion by Joanne Flynn Black
A Guide for Blended Families by Donna Jean Kendrick
Burnt Gloveboxes (Vol. II) by Gina Ramsey
Free Spirit at Free Safety by Joe Zagorski
Gray Matter by Avery Volz
A Guide for Widowhood by Donna Jean Kendrick
Fourteen Stones by Kris Faatz
Smooth Sailing (2nd Ed.) by Cheri Andrews, Esq.
Juris Ex Machina by John W. Maly
The Knowing by Kimberly Patton
Thriving Through Cancer by Kelly Lutman
Burnt Gloveboxes (Vol. I) by Gina Ramsey
The Selfish Hour by Megan Weisheipl
Intuitive Languages by Nicole Meltzer
What Color Am I? by Sarah Patterson

Peace in Passing (2nd Ed.) by Maribeth Decker

Hang on Tight! by Suzanne Tregenza Moore

A Path of Oneness by Ellen Feldman

Loud Woman by Jill Celeste, MA

By a Thread by Nicolette Blanco

Your4Truths by Judy Kane

You, Me, and Anxiety series by Dr. Robyn Reu Graham

That First Client (2nd Ed.) by Jill Celeste

You've Written Your Book. Now What? by Deborah Kevin

The Gift of Loss by Cathy Agasar

30 Second Success by Laura Templeton

CHILDREN'S TITLES

Betty Bartholomew and the Vanishing Begonias by Connie Jo Miller

Sara Smitherson and the Disappearing Snickerdoodles by Connie Jo Miller

Penelope Parsons and the Missing Pomegranates by Connie Jo Miller

My Body Knows. Do I Know? by Ashley Cournoyer-Smith

Meatball and Birdie by Elle Fox

Glitter Bird by Angie Bird

Lauren and Val Take a Walk by Lauren Eileen

FORTHCOMING TITLES

Animal Mayhem Burnt Gloveboxes (Vol. III) by Gina Ramsey

Unbreakable Us by Joëlle Lydon

The Divorce Money Map Workbook by Donna Jean Kendrick

Ripples on the Church Water by Brynn MacDonald

www.ingramcontent.com/pod-product-compliance
Lightning Source LLC
Chambersburg PA
CBHW051321120626
46547CB00015B/2334